COMING
TO
AMERICA

COMING
TO
AMERICA
Immigrants from NORTHERN EUROPE

ALBERT ROBBINS

DELACORTE PRESS / NEW YORK

Published by
Delacorte Press
1 Dag Hammarskjold Plaza
New York, N.Y. 10017

Manufactured in the United States of America
First printing

Picture research by Anne Phalon

Designed by Rhea Braunstein

LIBRARY OF CONGRESS CATALOGING IN PUBLICATION DATA

Robbins, Albert.
    Coming to America, immigrants from Northern
Europe.

    Bibliography: p.
    Includes index.
    SUMMARY: Discusses the experiences of immigrants
from France, Germany, the Netherlands, and Scandinavia
to the United States. Includes a chronology of U.S.
immigration laws.
        1. European Americans—History—Juvenile literature.
2. United States—Ethnic relations—Juvenile literature.
3. United States—Emigration and immigration—
Juvenile literature. [1. European Americans—History.
2. United States—Ethnic relations. 3. United States
—Emigration and immigration.] I. Title.
E184.E95R6   973'.04   80–68741
ISBN 0–440–01335–6

Contents

Introduction

Northern Europeans—people from the countries of France, Germany, the Netherlands, and Scandinavia —have been immigrating to America since the early seventeenth century when the Dutch first established a colony in present-day New York. Over the decades, millions of people from these lands came to find religious freedom, to seek better economic opportunities, and to seek refuge from periodic European strife. All brought some part of their culture and heritage with them. In the seventeenth and eighteenth centuries, they were in the minority in a land that was settled primarily by people from the British Isles. In the nineteenth century, when the majority of European immigrants arrived in America, they settled America's interior and helped build the nation's industries.

The descendants of northern European immigrants are so much a part of our country today that it is hard to imagine what the experience of the original settlers was like. Enough evidence is left behind, though—diaries, memoirs, newspapers, letters, and books—to piece the story together. None of the northern Europeans spoke English as a native language. And, far from the country they were raised in, they had to start new lives for themselves, often under severe conditions.

Northern European immigrants often had to deal with ethnic prejudice as cruel as that confronting new immigrants to America today. They had to adjust to a legal system that was unfamiliar to them. They had to learn American customs and manners. They had to discover the land itself, often much different from the mountains of Scandinavia, the forests of Germany, and the valleys of France. And most important of all, they had to discover what it meant to be in America, what it meant to become an American.

All this the immigrants did, not always in the first generation, but over the course of time. What happened to these people is called the process of assimilation—fitting into the society and culture around them. Northern Europeans, in some ways so much like the Anglo-Saxon majority in the United States, had an easier time than other immigrant groups in making the change. Yet it was also more difficult for them, because in addition to pioneering the land, they were also pioneers in forging one nation out of a mixture of very different kinds of people.

Ultimately the story of northern European immigrants to the United States is a success story. They made the difficult transition from the Old World to the New, becoming an integral part of the new country. It is a measure of their success that when Congress passed a law restricting immigration in the 1920s, the northern European countries, along with the British Isles, were favored. The fact that Congress put severe limits on immigration was shameful, but the law still shows the degree to which northern Europeans had become an accepted part of American society.

Northern European immigrants made important and valuable contributions to America. They settled the farmlands and the cities. They helped to build the railroads, canals, and highways. They served in every American war, became government officials, important intellectuals, and leading businessmen. Finally, they became so much a part of the mainstream in America that they lost the identification that American society imposed on the immigrant. They became simply, Americans, a vital part of the life of the nation.

Chapter 1

Explorers and Visionaries

Columbus's discovery of the New World in 1492 set off a phenomenon that was unique in human history. Imagine *Voyager 9* pointing its camera lenses at Saturn and finding not a dead landscape, enclosed in a poisoned atmosphere, but a verdant planet, much like Earth, inhabited by friendly peoples willing to show newcomers how to survive in this strange new environment, ready to be taken if only mankind could find the vehicles to transport settlers. Columbus's news had that effect on the European mind.

A new world! The idea inflamed the imagination of Europeans and held out to their densely populated kingdoms and duchies the possibility of starting afresh. Some people spoke of discovering great wealth. Some spoke of founding vast empires. Others, moved by the piety of the Reformation,

1

dreamed of founding perfect communities, rooted in the moral precepts of God.

Spain and Portugal took the lead in establishing colonies in the New World. The Spaniards encountered two great and rich Indian empires—the Aztecs and the Incas—whose wealth, which they plundered ruthlessly, served to incite the European quest for New World settlements even further. In 1493, shortly after Columbus returned to Spain from his first voyage of discovery, Pope Alexander VI issued a document called the *Bull Inter Caetera,* which divided the New World, as it was then becoming known, between Spain and Portugal. Pope Alexander was a Spaniard himself, and his closing off of the New World to the nations of northern Europe added to their resentment against the Catholic Church. England, France, Holland, and Sweden chose to ignore the papal order, and to carry out their own plans for the New World colonization.

In 1496 John Cabot, a Venetian mariner, applied to King Henry VII of England for a patent allowing him to explore the New World. He sailed the following year, on a small ship named *Matthew* with a crew of eighteen sailors, and established England's claim to North America. Another Italian explorer, Giovanni da Verrazzano, sailed to the New World for King Francis I of France in 1524. Verrazzano sailed by almost the entire coastline of North America, discovered New York Harbor (where a bridge today commemorates his feat), and laid claim to much of the area for France.

There was no independent Dutch nation in 1492. Holland was part of the Spanish Empire, and prospered by selling Spanish-manufactured goods throughout Europe. Then Protestantism swept the Low Countries in the mid-sixteenth century, and the Dutch people began a long struggle against their Catholic Spanish masters. The Dutch declared their independence from Spain in 1581 and acted as a free people, even though Spain did not formally recognize Dutch independence until 1648.

Holland was a maritime nation and depended on its ships to make the nation prosper. In the sixteenth century Spanish cargoes from the New World helped to fill Dutch ships, and commerce in New World goods became important for Holland's economy. Ironically, Holland's claim to lands in the New World was established in an effort to find a western sea route to Asia.

In 1609 the Dutch East India Company, a joint-stock company much like a modern business corporation, established to trade in the riches from Asia, hired an English mariner, Henry Hudson, to look for a shorter route to Asia. Hudson sailed to North America in his ship, *The Half-Moon*. He entered the river which today bears his name in the mistaken belief that it was a sea lane to Asia, and sailed as far north as what is today Albany, New York. Realizing that he had found a majestic river, not a route to the East, Hudson carefully surveyed his find and duly reported on it to his employers.

The East India Company lost no time in staking

out its claim to Hudson's "North River." In 1613 Adriaen Block mapped the coast of Long Island and New England as far east as the island off Rhode Island that bears his name, claiming all that he surveyed for the company. Block's colleague, Cornelis May, made a similar expedition the following year, claiming the lands as far south as Cape May, New Jersey.

The Dutch East India Company was more interested in trade than settlement. While it established trading posts in New York City, which the company called New Amsterdam, and in Albany, which it called Fort Orange, the company waited almost twenty years before encouraging permanent settlement on its lands. Instead, its activities in America centered on barter with Indians and the plunder of its hated enemy, Spain. An account of a Dutch fleet's attack on Spanish shipping in the 1620s illustrates how Dutch energies in the New World were put to use:

> The damage done . . . to our enemies, is easily estimated. We have, moreover, captured some even of the King of Spain's galleons, hitherto considered invincible. . . .
>
> Our ships and fleets also reduced, and for a time kept possession of, the rich and mighty city of St. Salvador, in Brazil; sacked Porto Rico; pointed out the way to seize its exceedingly enclosed harbors, and have destroyed the castle of Margrita.

By all which acts have we not only drained the King of Spain's treasury, but also further pursued him at considerable expense.[1]

The Dutch parliament, called the States General, chartered a new company called the Dutch West India Company in 1621 to begin settlements in New Netherland, as the colony based on Manhattan Island was called. The first group of settlers to come to the Dutch colony under the auspices of the new company arrived in New Amsterdam in 1624. Two years later, Pieter Jansen Schagen, a West India Company agent, was able to send back this glowing report from Amsterdam to his superiors in The Hague about the progress the colonists were making:

Here arrived yesterday the ship *The Arms of Amsterdam* which sailed from New Netherland out of the Mauritius [Hudson] River on September 23; they report that our people there are of good courage, and live peaceably. Their women, also, have borne children there, they have bought the island Manhattes from the wild men for the value of 60 guilders. . . . They sowed all their grain in the middle of May, and harvested it in the middle of August. . . . The cargo of the aforesaid ship is: 7246 beaver skins, 675 otter skins, 48 mink skins, 36 wild-cat skins, 33 mink, 34 rat skins. Many logs of oak and nut wood.[2]

Schagen's report is the only written record in existence of the most legendary real estate transaction of all time—the purchase of Manhattan Island for twenty-four dollars' worth of trinkets.

The Dutch settlers were considered to be servants of the West India Company rather than colonists. In 1629, in order to foster wider settlement in New Netherland, the company set up a feudal system of land under owners called *patroons* (Dutch for "patron" or "lord"). Under the patroon system, the company offered tracts of land along the Hudson to men of substance who were to recompense the Indians and establish a colony. They, in turn, were to finance settlement on their lands from Holland and receive certain tax exemptions and trading privileges. Only one patroonship or tract, Rensselaerwyck, set up by Kiliaen Van Rensselaer in 1630 near Fort Orange, was developed successfully. Others failed for a variety of reasons: mismanagement from absentee patroons, jealousies between the colonies and the New Netherland leadership, and lack of support from Holland, for land was so easy to acquire in the New World that the prospect of becoming a tenant on a patroon's property was not often appealing.

Because New Netherland was primarily a trading settlement, its population grew more slowly than that of other colonies. By 1646 it had only 1,500 inhabitants, compared to 25,000 English colonists in New England. That year the West India Company prohibited the establishment of new patroonships, opened New Netherland to all settlers, and offered to sell land, which it had not done before, for reasonable sums. As a result many more farmers, attracted by the prospect of buying inexpensive land, migrated to New Netherland, but the population of the colony never approached that of the English settlements.

Because New Netherland was primarily a trading colony, its relations with the local native Americans, whom the Dutch called *Wilden,* or "wild men," were relatively peaceful. New Netherland's major export was furs, especially beaver pelts, and Dutch traders bartered up and down the Hudson River for skins from the Algonquian tribes. By the 1630s Wouter Van Twiller, the Governor of New Netherland, estimated this trade in furs to be 7,500 pelts annually.

Dutch farmers in New Netherland tended to import their farming methods from the old country, in contrast to English settlers in New England who sought to learn from the native Americans everything they could about local agriculture, as well as hunting and fishing. The Dutch preferred to remain apart from the "wild men." And as long as the number of Dutch farmers in New Netherland remained small, the settlers lived peacefully with the native Americans. When large numbers of new settlers arrived in the 1640s, however, a series of bloody Indian wars broke out, and the Dutch drove most of the native Americans from the lower Hudson Valley.

In 1637 the Dutch were confronted with a

challenge to their colony from an unexpected source
—Sweden. That year, primarily through the efforts
of Willem Usselinx, one of the original promoters of
the Dutch West India Company, Queen Christina
of Sweden chartered the New Sweden Company. A
group of 50 settlers, under the direction of Peter
Minuit, a former Dutch official in New Netherland,
were sent to establish a colony on the Delaware
River.

New Sweden never attracted more than 250
settlers, mostly Finns, but it was irksome to the
Dutch. In 1645 Andreas Hudde, a Dutch spy, sent
back the following report on the Swedish colony to
his superiors in New Amsterdam:

> What regards the garrisons of the Swedes on
> the South-River [Delaware River] of New-
> Netherland is as follows:
> At the entrance of this River three leagues
> up from its mouth, on the east shore, is a fort
> called Elsenburgh, usually garrisoned by 12
> men and one lieutenant, 4 guns, iron and brass,
> of 12 pounds iron (balls), 1 mortar (*pots-
> hooft*). This fort . . . holds the river locked . . .
> so that all vessels, no matter to whom they
> belong or whence they come, are compelled to
> anchor there.
> About 3 leagues farther up the river is
> another fort, called Kristina, on the west side
> on a kil [creek] called Minquase Kil, so named
> because it runs very near to the Minquase [an

Indian tribe] land. . . . This fort has no permanent garrison but is pretty well provided and is the principal place of trade, where the Commissary also resides.[3]

Hudde went on to detail virtually every inhabitant, outbuilding, and farm in the Swedish colony. Then, in a comment that must have provoked some irate outbursts among the trade-conscious Dutch, he noted:

As regards the Schuykil, that is, the Hon. [Dutch West India] Company's purchased and possessed lands, [the Swedes have] destroyed the Hon. Company's timber and have built a fort at the place, on a very convenient island at the edge of the kil. . . . Fine corn has been raised on this island.[4]

What provocation! Destroying Dutch timber and growing fine corn on Dutch-owned land! The Dutch West India Company did not take kindly to this impertinence. In 1655 the Dutch sent a fleet up the Delaware—aided in no small part by Hudde's intelligence information—and conquered New Sweden. The small, short-lived settlement did make one lasting contribution to the American wilderness: Finnish woodsmen introduced an architectural innovation that generations of Americans would come to know as the log cabin.

Like the Dutch, French efforts to establish colonies in North America were geared more toward commerce than settlement. A French Huguenot sailor named Jean Ribaut established two colonies in the 1550s aimed at challenging Spanish rule in the Caribbean: one near present-day Beaufort, South Carolina, and another near Jacksonville, Florida. The colonies were smashed by a Spanish fleet after a few years, and Ribaut was massacred along with hundreds of his men.

Fifteen hundred miles to the north, the French were slightly more successful. In 1534 Jacques Cartier, a sea captain from St. Malo, set out for North America to uncover riches as fabulous as those the Spanish had found in Mexico. While he failed to achieve his goal, Cartier did explore the mouth of the St. Lawrence River, bringing back to France tales of extensive Indian cities along the river. In two successive voyages, the last made in 1542, Cartier sailed the length of the St. Lawrence and scouted the sites of present-day Quebec and Montreal. His attempts to found a French colony, however, like his search for gold, ended in failure.

Sixty years later a Frenchman named Samuel de Champlain succeeded where Cartier had failed. Champlain sailed the St. Lawrence in 1603, arriving at a trading post called Tadoussac, where he made an alliance with the Algonquian Indians which was to be instrumental in securing a French power base in Canada. Five years later, Champlain founded the city of Quebec, the first permanent French colony in North America.

The French were great frontiersmen who, despite their small numbers, ranged far and wide through the wilderness. By 1620, when the Pilgrims arrived in Massachusetts, French traders on the frontier, called *coureurs de bois,* had explored the St. Lawrence, discovered three of the Great Lakes, and traveled down the Susquehanna to the Chesapeake Bay. In the years to follow, French traders further extended their country's presence in North America by establishing outposts at Detroit, along the mid-Mississippi at St. Louis, and at New Orleans.

Although it was a vast territory, New France never attracted a large number of colonists. French colonial policy prohibited Protestants from settling in New France, and only Catholics, most of whom were reluctant to leave the Old World, were allowed to emigrate. Yet it was precisely because New France was Catholic that its size became so great. Catholic missionaries, mainly Jesuits, set out for the wilderness to convert the Indians with far greater zeal than their Protestant counterparts in the English colonies, and so established French claims to America's vast heartland.

While the French were busy expanding their holdings in North America, the English were equally forceful in consolidating theirs. The British had never recognized the Dutch claim to New Netherland, asserting that their own right to the territory, established by Cabot's voyages of discovery, predated Henry Hudson's claim by over one hundred years. To the British, the Dutch were trespassers to whom they allowed squatter's status. The Dutch were regarded as mere traders who could be ejected at will.

Dutch settlers in New Netherland, especially after the Dutch West India Company relaxed colonization rules in 1646, grew increasingly impatient with their rulers, who were appointed by the company and served the company's interests. In 1652 a group of settlers petitioned New Amsterdam Governor Peter Stuyvesant for some say in local affairs after a particularly bloody Indian uprising had occurred on Long Island. Stuyvesant's reply came to characterize the sort of despotism that the Dutch West India Company practiced in New Netherland:

> We derive our authority from God and company, not from a few ignorant subjects. If the nomination and election of magistrates were to be left to the populace, who were the most interested, then each would vote for one of his own stamp—the thief for a thief; the rogue, the tippler, the smuggler, for a brother in iniquity, that he might enjoy greater latitude in his vices and frauds.[5]

By 1664, after years of minor fights between English and Dutch settlers, the Dutch West India Company was in a poor position to defend itself. New Amsterdam had a population of only 1,600 and New Netherland as a whole only 10,000, many fewer than the New England colonies. In addition, the high-handedness of the company's rule had alienated many settlers who resented not having a say in their own affairs.

On March 12, 1664, King Charles II of England decided that his colonies could no longer tolerate the presence of the Dutch in North America. He granted title to the lands claimed by the Dutch to his brother James, the duke of York, and sent a fleet of four ships, commanded by Colonel Richard Nicolls, to conquer New Netherland. Nicolls reached New Amsterdam in August. He told the people of New Netherland that if they surrendered to the English, he would guarantee them the same rights that English colonists enjoyed—freedom of conscience, trading rights—and he guaranteed that the new English rulers would respect Dutch customs.

Despite violent protests from Governor Stuyvesant and other company officials, the people of New Amsterdam surrendered to Nicolls without ever firing a shot. After fifty years of West India Company rule, the English offer sounded far superior to their current government's practices.

English claims to New Netherland were confirmed in the Treaty of Breda in 1667. With the end of Dutch rule, England consolidated its colonial empire in North America from Maine in the North to Georgia in the South. English government, English language, and English customs prevailed in the colonies, but its population included many people from the northern European countries who found English ways to be alien to them. To a certain extent, how these people adapted to the English colonial experience would test the character of the British colonies.

Chapter 2

Aliens in an English World

By 1665, the year after the English consolidated their colonies through the conquest of New Netherland, the twelve British colonies had already emerged as very different from one another (Georgia, the thirteenth American colony, wasn't founded until 1732). Some of the colonies welcomed northern European immigrants, while others discouraged foreign settlers by forcing them to conform to strict laws that governed religion, dress, and land ownership. Only one colony, New York, had a large population of non-English-speaking people, the Dutch citizens of New Netherland.

There were three kinds of British colonies in America: commonwealths, proprietorships, and royal colonies. Commonwealths were permitted by the British to establish their own forms of government and to elect their own leaders. Proprietorships were outright grants of land made to wealthy and prominent Englishmen, but the proprietors usually gave their settlers some degree of self-government. Royal colonies were ruled by governors appointed by the king. These colonies generally elected some sort of self-governing legislative body, but their powers were mostly limited to advising the governor.

The way a colony was governed did not necessarily determine its attitudes toward non-English settlers. Massachusetts, a commonwealth, was ruled by Puritans who discouraged any people other than Puritans from living there; Rhode Island, another commonwealth, was much more liberal. Both Maryland and Pennsylvania, which were proprietorships, allowed religious freedom and encouraged immigration by all kinds of people; the Carolinas, a combined proprietorship until separated into North and South Carolina in 1712, were more restrictive. New York, a royal colony, was hospitable to different groups of newcomers, mainly because its large Dutch population made variety the norm.

The royal governors of New York did not attempt to force their Dutch citizens to adopt the English language and culture. In 1696 a royal charter declared:

> Our royal will and pleasure is, that no person in communion with the said Dutch Reformed Protestant Church within our city of New York, at any time, hereafter, shall be in any ways molested, punished, disquieted, or called into question for differences of opinion in matters

of the Protestant religion, who do not disturb
the civil peace of our said province. . . .[1]

Despite the fact that Dutch New Yorkers were
allowed to observe their native customs, English
rule, together with the ever-increasing number of
English-speaking colonists coming into New York,
made it inevitable that the Dutch would assimilate
eventually into the English mainstream.

Assimilation does not happen overnight. It is a
long process, carried on over generations. Writing in
1750, Peter Kalm, a European traveler to colonial
America, described how Dutch New Yorkers had
adjusted, after nearly a century, to English rule:

> Dutch was generally the language which was
> spoken in Albany. . . . and also in the places
> between Albany and New York [City] the pre-
> dominating language was Dutch. In New York
> [City] were also many homes in which Dutch
> was commonly spoken, especially by elderly
> people.
>
> The majority, however, who were of Dutch
> descent, were succumbing to the English
> language. The younger generation scarcely ever
> spoke anything but English, and there were
> many who became offended if they were taken
> for Dutch because they preferred to pass for
> English. . . . For this reason many deserted the
> Reformed and Presbyterian churches in favor
> of the English.[2]

Kalm noted that ethnic heritage gave way to English culture even more dramatically among American descendants of the much smaller group of settlers that made up New Sweden:

> We had a Swedish guide along who was probably born of Swedish parents, was married to a Swedish woman, but who could not, himself, speak Swedish. . . . Since English is the principle language of the land all people gradually get to speak that, and they become ashamed to talk in their own tongue because they fear they may not in such a case be real English. . . .
>
> Many Swedish women are married to Englishmen, and although they can speak Swedish very well it is impossible to make them do so, and when they are spoken to in Swedish, they always answer in English. . . .[3]

Assimilation is not a one-way street. Even though a group of people, over many generations, may become a part of the dominant culture, they still contribute some of their lost heritage to the mainstream. America's first great writer, Washington Irving, immortalized the Dutch of his native Hudson River Valley in his Knickerbocker's *History of New York,* written in the early nineteenth century. In one passage, describing a defense of New York City against Indian attack, Irving chronicled the great Dutch families of the Hudson valley, and, in his humorous way, attributed to each an identifying contribution to American culture:

First of all came the Van Brummels who inhabit the pleasant borders of the Bronx. . . .
They were the first inventors of suppawn, or
mush and milk. . . . After them came the Van
Pelts of Groodt Esopus . . . these were mighty
hunters of minks and musk rats, whence came
the word *Peltry.* Then the Van Nests of
Kinderhoeck, valiant robbers of birds' nests as
their name denotes. To these, if report may be
believed, are we indebted for the invention of
slap-jacks, or buckwheat cakes. . . .

Lastly came the KNICKERBOCKERS, of
the great town of Scaghtikoke, where the folk
lay stones upon the houses in windy weather,
lest they should be blown away. These derive
their names . . . from *Knicker,* to nod, and
Boeken, books: plainly meaning that they were
great nodders or dozers over books. . . .[4]

Irving, of course, was satirizing the Dutch
founders of his native valley. Yet his humor reflected an affectionate, even nostalgic, regard for
the Dutch, who, by Irving's time, had become
almost totally assimilated.

Even so, it was because New York still bore so
many Dutch characteristics, notably in architecture,
that Irving was inspired to write his tales. Today, in
New York City at least, the area's Dutch roots are
still evident in names like the Bronx (that borough
of New York City was originally the farm of Jonas
Bronck) and the Bowery (the Bouwerie was a farm

owned and operated by the Dutch West India Company). Dutch names have also played a part in our nation's history, most notably with the presidents of the United States who were descended from Dutch settlers: Martin Van Buren and Theodore and Franklin D. Roosevelt.

The eighteenth-century Dutch and Swedes in America were unique in that they were originally part of a settlement founded by their respective mother countries. After 1664 every non-English group of settlers who came to America arrived on their own, cutting any official ties they had to their homelands. As a result, even more pressure to assimilate was placed on these new groups by the dominant Anglo-American majority.

The French Huguenots and the Walloons (from the southern part of what is today Belgium) emigrated to America in the late seventeenth and eighteenth centuries. These settlers were Protestants who left France rather than give in to an edict issued by King Louis XIV which outlawed their religion. Since New France was open only to Catholics, the Huguenots and Walloons went to the British colonies. The French Protestants comprised only about five percent of France's population, but they were wealthy and well-organized. And as an official decree made clear, they had no choice but to flee France:

> If it happen again to be possible to fall upon such [Huguenot and Walloon] gatherings, let

orders be given to the dragoons to kill the greatest part of the Protestants that can be overtaken, without sparing the women, to the end that this may intimidate them and prevent others from falling into a similar fault.[5]

The French Protestants had to choose between converting to Catholicism or fleeing, and most chose flight. Because it was against the law for them to leave France, Huguenots and Walloons had to smuggle themselves out by bribing border guards or using false passports. It was expensive to escape from France and pay for a voyage to America. As a result a large percentage of the Huguenots and Walloons who came to the British colonies were well-to-do and skilled.

Most French Protestant immigrants eagerly embraced their new homeland and changed their names to make them sound more English—Paul Revere's father, for example, was named Appolos DeRivoire. In all, about fifteen thousand Huguenots and Walloons came to America, but despite their small numbers, their influence was widely felt. This was especially true in cities such as Boston, New York, Philadelphia, and Charleston, where their skills as craftsmen and merchants brought them wealth and influence.

Of all the British colonies, Pennsylvania was probably the most receptive to non-English immigration. In 1681, King Charles II granted William Penn, a Quaker, proprietorship over the territory that comprises present-day Pennsylvania and Delaware. The king owed a large debt to the Penn family —Penn's father, a British admiral, commanded the fleet that conquered Spanish Jamaica for England —and the colony was given to the younger Penn in payment for that service to the crown.

As a member of the radical new religious sect of Quakerism, Penn was dedicated to the principle of brotherhood among men. He not only encouraged religious freedom in his colony, but he actively sought out religious minorities and poor farmers— especially in Germany—and urged them to emigrate to Pennsylvania en masse. "The poor are the hands and feet of the rich," Penn wrote in a 1681 pamphlet, "and to encourage them [to emigrate] is to promote the real benefit of the public . . . there is an abundance of these people in many parts of Europe extremely desirous of going to America."[6]

Penn's advertisements of a safe haven in the New World were very successful. By 1685 the population of Penn's colony reached eight thousand, and Penn wrote that these included "not only English, but also French, Dutch, Germans, Swedes, Finns, Danes, Scotch, and Irish."[7] Aware that people in Europe tended to be frightened of other nationalities and ethnic groups, Penn emphasized that his diverse colonists "live as one people."[8]

In the same pamphlet Penn went on to give his view of the role of government, which was extremely liberal for the seventeenth century. Government, wrote Penn:

is duty to the King, the preservation of the right of all, the suppression of vice, the encouragement of virtue and arts, with liberty to all people to worship almighty God according to their faith and persuasion.[9]

Penn's humane views even extended to the native Americans who, in most other colonies, were either killed off or forced to flee. Of the Indians in Pennsylvania, the proprietor wrote:

> We have lived together in great friendship. . . . Our humanity has obliged them so far, and they generally leave their guns at home . . . they offer us no affront, not so much as to one of our dogs; and if any of them break our laws, they submit to be punished by them.[10]

Penn's policy of maintaining peaceful relations with the Indian tribes in Pennsylvania through fair treatment lasted for nearly fifty years—a unique exception to the bloody relations that characterized most contacts between settlers and native Americans. Eventually, as settlement in Pennsylvania spread farther and farther west, the inevitable Indian wars broke out. By the mid-eighteenth century there was little difference between settler-Indian relations in Pennsylvania and the other colonies. Penn's achievement in establishing peaceful relations with the native Americans was so unusual in colonial history that even as Indian wars broke out, Benjamin West, one of America's first great painters, commemorated the past age of peaceful relations in his canvas *Penn's Treaty with the Indians,* which now hangs in the Philadelphia Academy of Fine Arts.

Through his enlightened policies William Penn managed to attract more non-English-speaking settlers to his colony than any other proprietor, royal governor, or commonwealth government. In a way Penn's Quaker beliefs and his active seeking out of immigrants created America's first melting pot. Pennsylvania, in the eighteenth century, became a great experiment. Could such a mixed group of people live with one another peacefully, and, despite their differences in language and background, forge a new society?

Chapter 3

From "Deutsch" to "Dutch"

We are so used to thinking of Germany as one of the major nations of the modern world that it may be surprising to learn that Germany did not exist as a unified country until 1871. Until that time, the region we call Germany was only a collection of independent states with separate governments, such as Bavaria, Saxony, Württemberg, Prussia, and others, many of which dated back to the Middle Ages. Each ruler taxed his subjects according to his own whim and also declared what the official religion of the state would be. As a result, many Germans were faced with crushing economic burdens and, if they did not adhere to the state religion, with often violent persecution.

Germany in the seventeenth century was ravaged by a series of long and bloody wars. As rival armies moved back and forth across the land, they burned cities, destroyed crops and livestock, and looted the

25

population. If a German was lucky enough to survive the fortunes of war, he often became the victim
of the starvation and disease that followed on the
heels of battle. Survivors, understandably, became
demoralized, and many came to believe that it made
little sense to grow crops or repair their farms because the armies would eventually return and destroy
them. In 1618, at the start of the Thirty Years' War,
for example, the population of all the German states
was estimated to be 21 million; by 1648, that
population had fallen to less than 13.5 million. "I
was born in war," one survivor of the conflict said
when it finally ended. "I have no home, no country,
and no friends, war is all my wealth and now whither
shall I go?"[1] For many, America provided an
answer.

Against this backdrop, William Penn's promise of
virgin land and a fresh start in Pennsylvania, free
from war, religious persecution, and high taxes,
seemed like a gift from heaven. Many Germans were
anxious to grasp for anything that offered a change
from their unfortunate lot, and looked hopefully
toward the New World as a kind of Promised Land.
As news of America spread throughout Germany,
more and more Germans made the long, often
dangerous journey to the colonies. By the time of
the American Revolution, it was estimated that there
were nearly 225,000 colonists from Germany or of
German descent in the country.

More than any other ethnic minority in colonial
America, Germans were split into many different

religious groups. In general there were two major divisions: the "church people" and the "sectarians." The church people belonged to either the Lutheran or the German Reformed church, while the sectarians were members of one of the many small religious sects that began in seventeenth-century Germany, such as the Amish, Mennonites, Moravians, and Dunkers.

German immigrants found nearly every colony attractive, except those in New England. But Pennsylvania—because of William Penn's efforts to get them to move there and his promises of religious freedom—was the most appealing of all. Germans moved to Penn's colony in such large numbers that they made up one third of the population by 1790. These Pennsylvania Dutch (so-called because of a mispronunciation of the word *Deutsch,* which means "German") did not want to assimilate into the American mainstream. They came instead to farm their land, raise their families, and worship in their own special ways.

The first group of Germans to emigrate to Pennsylvania was led by Francis Daniel Pastorius, who guided a group of Mennonites to Philadelphia shortly after William Penn was granted his proprietorship. They and the related Amish fled from Europe, where their strict, conservative form of Protestantism had brought persecution on them from the Reformation itself. On March 7, 1684, Pastorius sent an account of the fortunes of his band of settlers back to Germany:

I, Francis Daniel Pastorius, with the wish and concurrence of our Governor, [have] laid out and planned a new town, which we called Germantown or Germanopolis, in a very fine and fertile district, with plenty of springs of fresh water, being well supplied with oak, walnut and chestnut trees, and having besides excellent and abundant pasturage for the cattle. At the commencement, there were but twelve families of forty-one individuals, consisting mostly of German mechanics and weavers. . . .

Our German society have in this place now established a lucrative trade in woollen and linen goods, together with a large assortment of other useful and necessary articles, and have entrusted this extensive business to my own direction. . . . All those who still arrive, have to fall to work and swing the axe most vigorously, for wherever you turn the cry is, *Itur in antiquam sylvam*, nothing but endless forests; . . . To our successors, and others coming after us, we would say, that they must not only bring over money, but a firm determination to labour and make themselves useful to our infant colony. . . .[2]

To Germans who saw America as a refuge from the chaos of Europe, Pastorius's warning that it would take hard work to carve out a new home in America posed no problem. Money was another matter, however. Most Germans were too poor to pay their own way to America, and even among those who weren't, few had the additional money needed to support themselves once they arrived there.

Some unscrupulous merchants and ship captains tried to profit from the poverty of German immigrants by paying for their passage, and then selling the services of these people (usually for seven years) to the highest bidder once they reached America, in payment of the debt. These operators hired recruiting agents called "Newlanders," who posed as American settlers returning to Germany for a visit. Dressed in expensive clothing, they showed off their money and jewels to unsuspecting Germans, telling them that there was much more to be gained in America.

One observer of the Newlanders in action commented:

> They would convince that there are in America, none but Elysian fields abounding in products which require no labor; that the mountains are full of gold and silver; and that the wells and springs gush forth milk and honey, that he who goes there as a servant becomes a lord, as maid, a gracious lady, as a peasant, nobleman.[3]

The Newlanders' trade continued for many years, despite accounts warning about their underhanded methods. Henry Melchior Muhlenberg described what it was like for a poor German to arrive in Philadelphia and be sold into servitude:

Before debarking, passengers are examined by
a medical officer, whether they are free from
contagious diseases. . . . [For] the less fortunate
—*unbemittelte*—without means, the ship is a
mart. . . . Young and unmarried persons of
both sexes are sold first and their future condition depends much on their master's dis-
position, situation and rank in society. Married
people, widows, and the infirm are dull sale. If
they have children these are sold, and the
parent's fare charged to the children's account,
and the children are consequently obliged to
serve a longer time. Children are in this way
not infrequently separated forever from their
parents. . . .

Many of [these unfortunate parents] are
compelled through their poverty, to beg their
bread from door to door from their German
countrymen. The English usually close their
doors against them, through fear of infectious
diseases. These things cause one's heart to
bleed, to see and hear fellow mortals who had
been persuaded to leave a Christian country,
lamenting, weeping, wringing their hands in
sad despair. . . . Little did the parents anticipate
such things.[4]

Because of warnings like Muhlenberg's, the
colonies eventually took action against the Newlanders and the merchants who financed them. A
Maryland reform law, for example, declared that

the practice subjected German immigrants "to cruel and oppressive impositions by the masters of the vessels in which they arrive, and likewise by those to whom they become servants."[5] The law then went on to outlaw the abuse.

What was it like for a family of poor German immigrants, recruited by Newlanders, to travel to America? In an account written in 1750, Gottlieb Mittleberger described in great detail the horror and depravation many Germans experienced:

> This journey [from Germany to America] lasts from the beginning of May to the end of October, fully half a year, amid such hardships as no one is able to describe adequately with their misery. . . .
>
> During the voyage [from England to America] there is on board these ships terrible misery, stench, fumes, horror, vomiting, many kinds of sea-sickness, fever, dysentery, head-ache, heat, constipation, boils, scurvy, cancer, mouth-rot, and the like, all of which come from old and sharply salted food and meat, also from very bad and foul water, so that many die miserably.
>
> Add to this want of provisions, hunger, thirst, frost, heat, dampness, anxiety, want, afflictions and lamentations, together with other trouble, as . . . the lice abound so frightfully, especially on sick people, that they can be scraped off the body. The misery reaches

the climax when a gale rages for 2 or 3 nights
and days, so that every one believes that the
ship will go to the bottom with all human
beings on board. . . .[6]

The horrors aboard ship to America that Mittleberger describes were just the final trial in a series
of hurdles immigrants had to pass. The initial trip
up the Rhine River to Holland involved multiple toll
stations where many people spent much of their
money. Taking ship from Holland to England was
difficult and expensive. Customs duties, once the
immigrants reached England, were often so high
that the little money the immigrants had left was
eaten up.

Many Germans were stranded in England in this
fashion, and had no alternative but to sign servitude
agreements to get to America. The sea voyage to
Pennsylvania lasted from seven to twelve weeks, and
Mittleberger spared no detail in recounting just how
horrible the voyage could be:

No one can have an idea of the sufferings
which women in confinement have to bear with
innocent children on board these ships. Few of
this class escape with their lives; many a mother
is cast into the water with her child as soon as
she is dead. . . .

Children from 1 to 7 rarely survive the
voyage; and many a time parents are compelled to see their children miserably suffer and

die. . . . I witnessed such misery in no less than 32 children in our ship, all of whom were thrown into the sea. . . .

That most of the people get sick is not surprising, because, in addition to all other trials and hardships, warm food is served only three times a week. . . . The water which is served out on the ships is often very black, thick and full of worms, so that one cannot drink it without loathing, even with the greatest thirst. . . . Towards the end [of the voyage] we were compelled to eat the ship's biscuit which had been spoiled long ago; though in a whole biscuit there was scarcely a piece the size of a dollar that had not been full of red worms and spiders' nests. . . .[7]

Despite the awful hardships of the trip to Pennsylvania, once a ship reached Philadelphia a poor German, probably sick and near starving, had no assurance that his ordeal was over. As Mittleberger pointed out:

When the ships have landed in Philadelphia after their long voyage, no one is permitted to leave them except those who pay for their passage . . . the others, who cannot pay, must remain on board the ships till they are purchased. . . . The sick always fare the worst, for the healthy are naturally preferred and purchased first; and so the sick and wretched must

> often remain on board in front of the city for
> 2 or 3 weeks, and frequently die, whereas
> many a one, if he could pay his debt and were
> permitted to leave the ship immediately, might
> recover and remain alive. . . .[8]

In spite of accounts like Mittleberger's—and
many just like it were circulated in Germany in the
seventeenth and eighteenth centuries—vast numbers
of Germans came to Pennsylvania. The dangers of
the ocean voyage, the exploitation of the Newlanders, and the cruelty those sold into servitude
endured could not diminish one basic fact—that
most German immigrants who survived found that
their lives in America were better than they had
been in Germany.

Like most eighteenth-century immigrants, the
Germans were mostly farmers. But unlike most
colonial farmers, who used their land carelessly and
often moved on when it was no longer fruitful,
Germans cultivated their land carefully, gaining a
reputation for being the best farmers in colonial
America. Dr. Benjamin Rush, a signer of the
Declaration of Independence, held German agriculture in particularly high esteem. In a pamphlet on
the subject, he wrote:

> The Germans, taken as a body, especially as
> farmers, are not only industrious and frugal,
> but skillful cultivators of the earth. . . . In
> settling a tract of land, they always provide

large and suitable accommodation for their horses and cattle, before they lay out much money in building a house for themselves. . . . The first dwelling house upon this farm is small and built of logs. It generally lasts the lifetime of the first settler of a tract of land; and hence, they have a saying, that "a son should always begin his improvements where his father left off," that is by building a large and convenient stone house. . . .[9]

After describing the marvels of the German farmhouse, Dr. Rush went on to enumerate the wonders of the German farm itself:

They feed their horses and cows well, of which they keep only a small number, in such a manner that the former perform twice the labor of those horses, and the latter yield twice the quantity of milk of those cows, that are less plentifully fed. . . .

The fences of a German farm are generally high and well built, so that his fields seldom suffer from the inroads of his own or his neighbors' horses, cattle, hogs, or sheep. . . .

The German farmers are great economists in their wood. Hence they burn it only in stoves, in which they consume but a fourth or fifth of what is commonly burnt in ordinary open fireplaces. . . .[10]

To Dr. Rush, perhaps the greatest wonder of all was the German farmer's attitude toward his family. In a time when families were usually large, and new mouths to feed were often dreaded, the German farmer, according to Rush, took quite a different attitude:

> The German farmers live frugally in their families, with respect to diet, furniture and apparel. They sell their most profitable grain . . . and eat that which is less profitable. . . . The profit to a farmer, from this single article of economy, is equal, in the course of a lifetime, to the price of a farm for one of his children. . . .
>
> The favorable influence of agriculture, as conducted by the Germans, in extending human happiness, is manifested by the joy they express upon the birth of a child. No dread of poverty, nor distrust of Providence, from an increasing family depresses the spirit of these industrious and frugal people. Upon the birth of a son, they exult in the gift of a plowman or a wagoner; and upon the birth of a daughter, they rejoice in the addition of another spinster or milkmaid to the family.[11]

The tendency of Germans to concentrate in certain areas made it possible for them to preserve their distinctive language and culture longer than most other immigrants. In fact, some groups—

especially those in southeastern Pennsylvania, the people we today refer to as Pennsylvania Dutch— are not very much different from their colonial forebears who settled there. The Amish, or Plain People, in particular, still preserve the seventeenth-century German or Swiss culture of their ancestors. Even today they dress simply, reject many modern conveniences such as the automobile, often maintain their own schools, and in some churches retain German for religious services.

Yet the colonial Germans posed a unique problem to the dominant English-speaking majority in Pennsylvania and the other colonies. Because they isolated themselves, they had little opportunity to assimilate; indeed, they actively fought against the erosion of German culture. As a result, the English-speaking colonists came to mistrust the Germans, and some, including even such a freethinking person as Benjamin Franklin, came to look upon them as foreign, as outsiders, people who didn't belong in America.

In a letter he wrote in May 1753, Franklin outlined his views about Germans to a friend:

> Few of their children in the country know English. They import many books from Germany; and of the six printing-houses in the province, two are entirely German, two half-German half-English, and but two entirely English. . . . Advertisements, intended to be

general, are now printed in [Pennsylvania] Dutch and English. The signs in our streets have inscriptions in both languages, and in some places only German. They begin of late to make all of their bonds and other legal instruments in their own language which (though I think it ought not to be) are allowed good in our courts . . . and I suppose in a few years [interpreters] will be necessary in the Assembly, to tell one half of our legislators what the other half say.

They [may] soon so outnumber us that all the advantages we have will, in my opinion, be not able to preserve our language, and even our government will become precarious.[12]

The view Franklin was expressing, which later in the nation's history came to be called *nativism,* was a divisive one. It was based on the idea of first come, first served—that somehow the original colonists and their descendants deserved preferred treatment over latecomers, and that no foreign culture should be permitted to compete with the society established by those who were here first.

To a degree, the roots of nativism are easy to understand. Most people resist change. Anything that threatens to alter what they're used to is viewed with suspicion. Franklin's comments, coming barely twenty years before the American Revolution, identified a problem that was to plague American society to the present. Despite Franklin's hostility, no overt action was taken in Pennsylvania to deprive the German settlers of their right to their own language and culture. In later periods, however, the same did not always hold true for other ethnic groups who came to America.

Chapter 4

A New Nation

By the mid-eighteenth century, the British colonies in North America had become very different from England. The existence of the vast American frontier gave colonists the freedom to move to new, unsettled lands far from the centers of colonial government. This mobility bred a spirit of independence in the American colonists that triggered the chain of events that led to the American revolution.

In 1763, following the Seven Years' War with France, the British and French governments signed the Treaty of Paris, which gave Britain all the French territory in North America, except for two small islands off the coast of eastern Canada. As a result, England found itself in possession of nearly all the territory east of the Mississippi River. The American colonists, who had fought long and hard against the French, naturally expected that the royal government would open up the newly acquired lands to settlement. But in the Proclamation of 1763, the British crown decreed that settlers could not inhabit any of the western lands.

The British policy of limiting western settlement stirred considerable resentment in the colonies. Since many of the settlers on the frontier were northern Europeans, mostly Germans, they inevitably became caught up in the controversy. At the same time, a series of laws passed by the British Parliament—mainly tax laws like the Stamp Act of 1765 and the Tea Act of 1773—created a serious crisis that grew into active rebellion against the British.

The issues that led to the American revolution were alien to most German-, French-, and Scandinavian-born settlers in the British colonies. The English colonists regarded the royal decrees and acts of Parliament aimed at them as laws that took away their rights as Englishmen—rights that traditionally included freedom of movement and representation in Parliament. Most northern Europeans in the colonies, particularly Germans, who made up the largest ethnic group outside of the British in North America, came from countries that had no similar tradition.

Germans came from states where they had no rights of participation in government at all. Most Germans in colonial America spoke only their native tongue and could not even engage in political discussions with their English-speaking neighbors. Many of the repressive laws, like the tax on tea, really had no effect on German settlers because they, unlike the British, were not in the habit of drinking tea day in and day out.

Nevertheless, Germans flocked to the cause of American independence. In part their hostility toward the British crown was due to the closing off of the western frontier. But the most important factor was the tax Germans were forced to pay to support the Church of England.

Today freedom of religion is guaranteed by the First Amendment to the Constitution, but people in colonial America had to pay a tax to support the official church, whether they were members of the church or not. This meant that the Germans, nearly all of whom were religious people who had come to America to practice various forms of Protestantism, had to give money to the English church as well as their own.

In 1765 Benjamin Franklin appeared before the British Parliament to explain colonial opposition to the stamp tax. Asked by one member if the Germans in his native Pennsylvania were as opposed to the tax as other colonists, Franklin replied:

> Yes, even more [than Anglo-Americans] and they are justified because in many cases they must pay double for their stamp-paper and parchments.[1]

That sort of discrimination, coupled with the support Germans had to pay for the Church of England, made them an important element in the revolution against British rule.

When the Revolution began, nearly every German-American minister in the colonies declared himself in favor of the cause of independence. This had an enormous effect on churchgoing Germans, and many all-German regiments for the Continental army were raised through the German churches. In January 1776, for example, Peter Muhlenberg, a Lutheran minister in Woodstock, Virginia, enlisted more than three hundred recruits from his congregation with a particularly moving sermon. He proclaimed:

> In the language of holy writ, there was a time for all things, a time to preach, and a time to pray, but those times had passed away; that there was a time to fight, and that time had now come![2]

Concluding his sermon, Muhlenberg tore off his ministerial robes to show the Continental army uniform he was wearing. He went on to distinguish himself as a general in the Revolutionary army.

Other German-Americans became heroes of the Revolutionary War as well. Perhaps the most important of them was Baron Friedrich Wilhelm von Steuben. He was born in Prussia and served as an officer in the Prussian army. Shortly after the Revolution began, von Steuben met Benjamin Franklin in Paris. Franklin recruited the Prussian officer to the American cause and wrote a letter of introduction for him to George Washington.

General Washington was impressed by von Steuben's background. At Washington's urging, the Continental Congress made von Steuben the Inspector General of Washington's army, in charge of drilling the troops to create tighter discipline. Von Steuben was so successful in this that by the end of the war one observer commented that the Continentals "seemed in danger of becoming an overseas branch of the Prussian army."[3] Von Steuben played a major part in Washington's ultimate victory, and his name is still revered in the German-American community, in annual Steuben Day celebrations, as one of America's founding fathers.

Two other German-American generals distinguished themselves in the Revolution. One, Brigadier General Nicolaus Herkimer, played an instrumental part in the war in upstate New York, especially in the Mohawk Valley, which was a center for German settlement. Another, Baron Johann de Kalb, was made a major general in the Continental army by Washington. At the Battle of Camden, South Carolina, in 1780, his outnumbered German regiment stood and fought the British in a losing cause, allowing other American forces to retreat successfully. De Kalb, wounded eleven times, was killed in the battle.

George Washington was aware of the bravery and loyalty of German-American troops in the Continental army. In 1776, after he began to suspect that his personal troop of bodyguards had been infiltrated by Tory spies, Washington disbanded his English-speaking troop, replacing it with an all-German unit. The new troop, called the Independent Troop of Horse, was made up entirely of German-Americans recruited in Pennsylvania. It served as Washington's personal bodyguard until the end of the war.

Germans fought on the British side in the Revolution also, but these soldiers were mercenaries, imported from Germany, who fought not out of loyalty to a cause, but for the money the British paid them. Called Hessians, because most of them came from the German state of Hesse, these soldiers had no particular loyalty to the British. In fact, after Washington captured a large number of Hessians in the Battle of Trenton, he sought to recruit them to the American cause by taking them to the German-speaking areas of Pennsylvania, where the German soldiers could converse in their own language with German-American patriots. By the end of the Revolution, nearly 12,000 of the 30,000 Hessians the British sent to the colonies had defected to the American cause.

Most of the French Huguenot settlers in the British colonies had become Americanized by the time of the Revolutionary War. Many of their descendants, such as Paul Revere, the Boston silversmith who sounded the alarm about the first battle of the war, were distinguished patriots. But European Frenchmen also played a key role in the

American Revolution. In fact most historians agree that the colonists could not have won the Revolution at all without the help given them by the French.

The Frenchman who did the most to help the American cause was the Marquis de Lafayette, who was a nineteen-year-old captain in the French army when he first heard the news of the American Revolution. Moved by the ideal of liberty, which French thinkers such as Jean Jacques Rousseau and Voltaire championed, Lafayette decided to join the Continental army. "At the first news of this quarrel," Lafayette wrote later in his life, "my heart was enrolled in it."[4]

Lafayette sailed for America late in 1776, and he was appointed a major general in Washington's army by the Continental Congress on July 31, 1777. Lafayette quickly distinguished himself on the battlefield, prompting General Washington to write to Congress urging them to give the young Frenchman command of an entire division:

> He is sensible, discreet in his manners, had made a great proficiency in our language, and from the disposition he discovered at the Battle of Brandywine, possesses a large share of bravery and military ardor.[5]

Lafayette's most important contribution to American independence, however, came not on the battlefield, but in his native France, where he was instrumental in convincing King Louis XVI's foreign minister, the Comte de Vergennes, to formally recognize the American republic and supply it with military aid. The French had been undecided about helping the Americans in their fight against France's traditional enemy, England, since the outbreak of the Revolution. American envoys to the French court, such as John Adams, had been unable to persuade the French to join the fight.

Early in 1778 news reached Paris of the American victory over the British in the Battle of Saratoga. American envoys used the news to negotiate a formal alliance with the American rebels, and France, joining in the fight against England, became the first European country to recognize the independence of the "United States of America." During the first year of the alliance, however, France supplied little help to the Americans.

Lafayette was dispatched to France to convince the French to supply more aid, especially enough naval aid to help defeat the British fleet. Lafayette asked the Comte de Vergennes to give the Americans "a decided naval superiority for the next campaign," explaining:

With a naval inferiority, it is impossible to make war in America. It is that which prevents us from attacking any point that might be carried with two or three thousand men. It is that which reduces us to defensive operations, as dangerous as they are humiliating. The

English are conscious of this truth, and all their
movements prove how much they desire to
retain the empire of the sea.[6]

Lafayette's pleas had their effect, and de
Vergennes dispatched a large fleet—under the
command of Admiral de Grasse—and a large land
force—commanded by the Count de Rochambeau—
to the American fight. On September 5, 1781, de
Grasse's French fleet defeated the British fleet at the
mouth of the Chesapeake Bay. The British fleet had
been attempting to come to the rescue of the large
British army under the command of General Cornwallis at Yorktown, Virginia. De Grasse's victory
enabled Washington and Rochambeau to continue
their siege at Yorktown, and on October 17, 1781,
General Cornwallis surrendered, ending the American Revolution. Two years later England signed a
peace treaty with the Americans in Paris. England
recognized the United States as an independent
country, and dropped its claims to territory south of
Canada and east of the Mississippi River.

Victory over the British created the American
nation. The early years of independence were
chaotic, and in 1787 a Constitutional Convention
met in Philadelphia to draft a new foundation for
governing the new country. One of the important
questions the delegates had to decide was how new
immigrants to the United States could become
citizens, and whether foreign-born citizens should
be allowed to serve in the new federal government.

In the debate over eligibility for election to the Senate and the House of Representatives, many delegates expressed fears that foreigners would undermine the new government if allowed to participate in it:

> Col. Mason [George Mason, delegate from Virginia] was for opening a wide door for emigrants; but did not chuse to let foreigners and adventurers make laws for us & govern us. . . . It might also happen that a rich foreign Nation, for example Great Britain, might send over her tools who might bribe their way into the Legislature for insidious purposes.
>
> Mr. Pinckney [Charles Pinckney, delegate from South Carolina, said] As the Senate is to have the power of making treaties & managing our foreign affairs, there is peculiar danger and impropriety in opening its door to those who have foreign attachments. He quoted the jealousy of the Athenians on this subject who made it death for any stranger to intrude his voice into their legislative proceedings.[7]

While these arguments reflected caution on the part of the delegates to foreign immigration to the United States, Gouverneur Morris of Pennsylvania went to an extreme in voicing his nativist views to the Convention:

> [Gouverneur Morris] ran over the privileges which emigrants would enjoy among us, though

they should be deprived of that of being eligible to the great offices of Government; . . . The men who can shake off their attachments to their own Country can never love any other. These attachments are the wholesome prejudices which uphold all Governments. Admit a Frenchman into your Senate, and he will study to increase the commerce of France: An Englishman, he will feel an equal bias in favor of that of England.[8]

These views were strongly refuted at the Convention, with many delegates arguing that America had been founded by immigrants and should adopt a liberal policy toward them in the future. Delegates from Pennsylvania Benjamin Franklin and James Wilson (himself an immigrant from Scotland) were especially outspoken in their views:

Docr. Franklin [said that] The people in Europe are friendly to this Country. Even in the Country with which we have been lately at war, We have now & had during the war, a great many friends, not only among the people at large, but in both Houses of Parliament. . . . We found in the Course of the Revolution that many strangers served us faithfully, and that many natives took part against their Country. When foreigners, after looking about for some other country in which they can obtain more happiness, give a preference to ours, it is a proof of attachment which ought to excite our confidence and affection.

Mr. Wilson . . . mentioning the circumstance of his not being a native . . . remarked the illiberal complexion which the motion would give to the System & the effect which a good system would have in inviting meritorious foreigners among us, and the discouragement & mortification they must feel from the degrading discrimination, now proposed.[9]

Ultimately the nativist and proimmigrant factions at the Constitutional Convention reached a compromise. For a candidate to be elected to the House of Representatives, the Constitution specified that he had to be a citizen of the United States for at least seven years; to be elected to the Senate, nine years; and to be elected President, he had to be a native-born citizen of the United States. The power to determine citizenship requirements for new immigrants was left to Congress.

The debate over foreign immigration to the United States and foreign-born citizens' ability to participate in the federal government reflected a division in American thinking that was to reappear again and again in the course of the nation's history. The same year that the Constitution was ratified, 1789, an event occurred in Europe that was to put American attitudes toward foreigners to their first important test. That event was the outbreak of the French Revolution.

Chapter 5

Isolated and Cut Off

The French Revolution broke out in the summer of 1789, just a few months after George Washington was inaugurated as first President of the United States. It set off an international upheaval that lasted for twenty-five years. In that time the nations of Europe were almost constantly at war with each other. The radical ideas of the Revolution threw the old order of Europe into chaos. Within a few years of the Revolution, Napoleon Bonaparte had turned Europe into a fortress that few could enter and from which fewer still could escape.

As a result immigration to the United States during the years 1789–1815 was practically zero. Some political refugees did make their way to the new American republic, mostly from France, but these newcomers were few in number. The isolation America experienced during this period caused the new nation to turn inward, to search for its own identity while absorbing the many foreign strains that had come earlier.

When news of the Revolution in France first reached the United States, it was greeted with great interest. Most Americans, mindful of their own revolutionary struggle against British tyranny, saw the uprising in France as an extension of the ideals that had led to American independence. As revolutionary fervor in France intensified, however, the horror of the "Reign of Terror"—in which radicals attempted to stamp out every remnant of the monarchy, guillotining thousands of people—upset many Americans who were revolted by what they perceived as a nation mired in anarchy.

American attitudes toward the French Revolution were put to the test in the early 1790s. France, like the United States, had declared itself to be a republic, and Great Britain had gone to war against the new French government. Because of the American-French alliance of 1778, the United States had to come to France's aid in any war against England. But the alliance had been signed with the government of King Louis XVI. Many officials of the American government were fearful that French extremism would spread to America if the United States honored its commitment, and they argued that the change in the French government altered America's obligation.

In April 1793 President Washington issued an official proclamation of American neutrality. The French, upset by the decree, sent an emissary,

"Citizen Genêt," to the United States to persuade the American people to help the French cause. Arriving in Charleston, South Carolina, Genêt immediately became a center of controversy. He chartered American privateers in the name of the French Republic to attack British shipping—a direct violation of American law. He also publicly attacked President Washington with such revolutionary fervor that the worst fears of the anti-French faction in America seemed to be coming true. Washington, in what became known as the "Genêt affair," ordered the outspoken revolutionary expelled from the United States.

Genêt's pleas did not fall on deaf ears, however. After it declared war on France, England seized hundreds of American merchant ships heading for French ports. These attacks, coupled with an unpopular treaty with England negotiated by Chief Justice John Jay in 1794, which seemed to acknowledge Britain's right to interfere with American shipping, aroused considerable anti-British sentiment. The United States soon found itself divided into two factions: a pro-British party headed by Treasury Secretary Alexander Hamilton and a pro-French party headed by Secretary of State Thomas Jefferson.

Neither Hamilton nor Jefferson wanted to involve the United States in the war between France and England, and both agreed with President Washington that the United States needed peace in order to establish the new nation on a firm footing. But

Hamilton saw America's future tied to that of England, while Jefferson was sympathetic to the ideas of the French Revolution, though revolted by its excesses.

The split between the two cabinet members led, informally at first, to the creation of America's two-party political system. Hamilton's faction, which became known as the Federalists, favored sound financial policy and industrial development. It included in its number most city dwellers and most of the affluent citizens. Jefferson's faction, the Democratic-Republicans (which is the forerunner of today's Democratic party) wanted to develop the country as a nation of small farms, rooted in democratic ideals which Jefferson saw as inherent in rural life. The Federalists favored a strong federal government, while the Democratic-Republicans advocated a decentralized national government that would leave most powers to the individual states.

Jefferson's democratic idealism did not extend to his attitude toward immigration. The author of the Declaration of Independence, like many Americans of his time, feared that a flow of foreigners to the United States would destroy its character. In his *Notes on Virginia* Jefferson wrote:

> But are there no inconveniences to be thrown into the scale against the advantage expected from a multiplication of numbers by the importation of foreigners? . . . Suppose twenty millions of republican Americans thrown all

of a sudden into France, what would be the condition of that kingdom? If it would be more turbulent, less happy, less strong, we may believe that the addition of half a million of foreigners to our present number would produce a similar effect here.

If they come of themselves they are entitled to all the rights of citizenship; but I doubt the expediency of inviting them by extraordinary encouragements. . . .[1]

One of the by-products of the development of the two-party system was the development of a lively American press. Both the Federalists and the Democratic-Republicans supported newspapers that passionately set forward the party's views. Jefferson's journalistic advocate was a fiery writer of Huguenot descent named Philip Freneau.

As a young man just prior to the American Revolution, Freneau attended Princeton University in New Jersey, where, along with his classmates James Madison, (Light Horse) Harry Lee (later Revolutionary cavalry leader and governor of Virginia, also father of Robert E. Lee), and Aaron Burr, he became an ardent advocate of the cause of American independence. At the outbreak of the Revolution, Freneau captained a small privateer that was captured by a British warship. Freneau was imprisoned by the British in a rotting hulk in New York Harbor that was used to incarcerate captured rebels. His health nearly ruined by the experience,

Freneau wrote an impassioned poem about it titled "The Prison Ship" that earned him the title "Poet of the American Revolution."

Freneau never forgave the British for what they had done to him, and he seemed a natural candidate to edit an anti-Federalist newspaper when his former classmate James Madison brought him to Jefferson's attention in 1791. Jefferson gave Freneau a small salary as a State Department translator, and began publishing his Democratic-Republican organ, the *National Gazette*. So sharp were Freneau's attacks on the Federalists that Alexander Hamilton personally published an attack against the editor, charging that he had no right to criticize the government that paid his salary. Freneau's reply is a classic example of the heated invective of the time:

The above is beyond reply. It might be queried, however, whether a man who receives a small stipend for services rendered as a French translator to the Department of State, and as editor of a free newspaper . . . is not more likely to act an honest and disinterested part toward the public, then a vile sycophant, who obtaining emoluments from government, far more lucrative than the salary alluded to, finds his interest in attempting to poison the minds of the people by propaganda and by disseminating principles and sentiments utterly subversive of the true republican interests of the country. . . .[2]

Freneau's sharply worded attacks and those of other Jeffersonian editors, together with the equally sharp responses of the Federalist press, served to intensify the rivalry between the two political parties. When George Washington's second term as President came to an end, Jefferson opposed John Adams in the election of 1796 and was defeated by a narrow margin. Under electoral rules of the time, Jefferson, as runner-up, became Vice-President under the Federalist Adams.

Jefferson seemed certain to succeed Adams as President in the next election. In 1797, however, an event occurred which aroused anti-French sentiment in America. A delegation of American commissioners was sent to France by President Adams to negotiate a new treaty. Three Frenchmen were sent by French Foreign Minister Talleyrand to meet the Americans, and these French agents, who became known in America as X, Y, and Z, demanded a huge bribe before treaty negotiations could begin. The Americans refused to pay the bribe, and they returned home without a treaty.

When the XYZ affair was made public, it infuriated the American people. "Millions for defense," declared a popular slogan of the day, "but not one cent for tribute!" Americans geared up for war with France, beginning a program to expand the navy dramatically. At the same time, foreigners living in the United States, especially French refugees from the Revolution, were suddenly looked upon as potential enemies who were a threat to "native" Americans.

President Adams proposed a series of controversial new laws to control the threat he perceived of potential enemies living in the United States. Called the Alien and Sedition Acts, these new laws challenged the delicate fabric of the Constitution that had been ratified only ten years earlier. One law, the Naturalization Act, increased the residence requirement to become an American citizen from five to fourteen years. Through this law, the administration effectively prevented any of the newly arrived refugees from enjoying the rights of citizenship, at least during the crisis. Another law, the Alien Act, gave the President broad powers to deal with foreigners:

> It shall be lawful for the President of the United States at any time . . . to order all such aliens as he shall judge dangerous to the peace and safety of the United States, or shall have reasonable grounds to suspect are concerned in any treasonable or secret machinations against the government thereof, to depart out of the territory of the United States.[3]

The law left the determination of whether or not an alien was "dangerous" entirely to the President. In order to keep track of foreigners, another provision of the law required sea captains to register any foreigners they brought into the country:

Every master or commander of any ship or
vessel which shall come into any port of the
United States . . . shall immediately, on his
arrival, make report in writing . . . of all aliens,
if any, on board his vessel, specifying their
names, age, the place of nativity, the country
from which they shall have come, the nation
to which they belong and owe allegiance, their
occupation, and a description of their persons.[4]

Compiling dossiers on foreigners entering the
United States seemed to go against the grain of the
principles on which the nation was founded. Some
defended the law as a necessary measure temporarily
enacted to protect the country at a time when war
seemed about to break out. The Sedition Act, however, passed at the same time as the Alien Act, was
criticized as no more than a partisan Federalist law
aimed at silencing the Democratic-Republican
opposition. The Sedition Act made it a crime to

write, print, utter, or publish, or . . . cause
or procure to be written, printed, uttered or
published . . . any false, scandalous and
malicious writing or writings against the
government of the United States, or either
house of Congress of the United States, or the
President of the United States with intent to
defame the said government . . . or to bring
them . . . into contempt or disrepute, or to
excite against them . . . the hatred of the good
people of the United States.[5]

The new laws immediately came under severe criticism. Jefferson's supporters charged that they violated constitutional guarantees of free speech, freedom of the press, and the right of the people to assemble freely. Democratic-Republican Edward Livingston summarized the danger of the laws in a speech before Congress:

> [The President] is not only authorized to make this law for his own conduct but to vary it at pleasure, as every gust of passion, every cloud of suspicion, shall agitate or darken his mind. The same power that formed the law, then, applies it to the guilty or innocent victim, whom his own suspicions, or the secret whisper of a spy, have designated as its object . . . This, then, comes completely within the definition of despotism.[6]

Instead of unifying the country behind the Federalists and undermining Jefferson's popularity, the Alien and Sedition Acts aroused public opinion against President Adams's administration. As Jeffersonian newspaper editors like Freneau were rounded up and jailed, along with any suspect foreigners, the possibility of the new Constitution being destroyed became very real. As a result, Jefferson was elected President in the election of 1800, and the Alien and Sedition Acts, which had been enacted for a two-year period, were allowed to expire by the new Jeffersonian majority in Congress.

In his First Annual Message to Congress, President Jefferson, aware that his election was in part due to opposition to the notorious Alien Act, proposed a more conciliatory policy toward foreign refugees:

> Shall we refuse the unhappy fugitives from distress that hospitality which the savages of the wilderness extended to our fathers arriving in this land? Shall oppressed humanity find no asylum on this globe? . . . Might not the general character and capabilities of a citizen be safely communicated to every one manifesting a bona fide purpose of embarking his life and fortunes permanently with us?[7]

While he was unaware of it at the time, a lucky chain of events during Jefferson's first term as President resulted in what, ultimately, would serve to attract millions of immigrants to America: the Louisiana Purchase. In 1803 Jefferson sent his friend James Monroe to France to try to purchase the port of New Orleans—essential to American commercial traffic on the Mississippi River—from France. Napoleon had acquired all of the Louisiana Territory through his conquest of Spain in 1801.

When Monroe arrived in Paris, he learned to his astonishment that Napoleon was willing to sell not only New Orleans but the entire Louisiana Territory, an area of land nearly as large as the United States at the time. Even though he was exceeding his authority, Monroe, together with the American ambassador to France, Robert Livingston, agreed to purchase the territory for 60 million francs, approximately $15 million. In one stroke of the pen, the size of the United States doubled.

Together with a sizable French-speaking population in what is today the state of Louisiana, the Louisiana Purchase brought with it immense areas of land inhabited mainly by the various Indian tribes of the Great Plains and the Rocky Mountains. The area of the Purchase territory was so great, in fact, that the United States government had only a vague idea of what it had acquired.

In 1805 President Jefferson dispatched two army officers, Meriwether Lewis and William Clark, to survey the Purchase territory and report back on its character. For more than a year the two explorers made their way across the United States, guided for much of the time by a Snake Indian woman named Sacajawea. She spoke a great variety of native American languages, a talent that proved invaluable to Lewis and Clark as they encountered tribes of Indians very few white men had ever met before: Sioux and Shawnee, Mandans and Pawnee, Creeks and Osage, Nez Percés and Chinooks. Lewis and Clark came in contact with a great variety of native American cultures. Oftentimes the Indians were perplexed by these strange newcomers, as a Shoshoni chief reported to Warren A. Ferris, an American Fur Company agent, decades later:

> They were unlike any people we had hitherto seen, fairer than ourselves, and clothed with

skins unknown to us. They seemed to be
descended from the regions of the great
"Edle-a-ma-hum." They gave us things like
solid water [mirrors], which were sometimes
as brilliant as the sun, and which sometimes
showed us our own faces. Nothing could equal
our wonder and delight. We thought them the
children of the Great Spirit.[8]

When Lewis and Clark returned from their
journey, which carried them from the Mississippi
River to the Pacific coast of Oregon and back, they
brought with them a wealth of information about
this new territory of the United States. Lewis and
Clark's tales of lush grasslands and virgin forests in
the present-day States of Iowa, Missouri, Arkansas,
Minnesota, Kansas, Nebraska, the Dakotas,
Colorado, Montana, and Oregon—all of which were
sparsely settled by the various tribes—proved to be
an irresistible lure to European farmers dreaming of
greener pastures in America. The movement of
settlement to the West that Lewis and Clark's report
helped to trigger would eventually result in the near
annihilation of native American culture in North
America.

As long as Europe was cut off by the Napoleonic
Wars, however, immigration remained almost non-
existent. Throughout the first decade of the nineteenth century, America remained isolated from
Europe. The isolation was formalized in 1807 by
the Embargo Act, which prohibited American

merchant ships from trading with any of the belligerent powers of Europe, a classification that included a large part of the continent, i.e., England, Russia, Prussia, Poland, Austria. The Embargo Act was brought about by stepped-up attacks on American shipping by both the British and the French.

The British went one step further in their attacks, however. Royal Navy ships stopped American vessels on the high seas and searched their crews for sailors they claimed were deserters from the Royal Navy. Many American sailors were forced to serve in the British navy as a result, and Congress reacted to the insult by declaring war on Great Britain in 1812.

The War of 1812, which lasted for nearly three years, isolated America from Europe even more. Where before the war American ships were attacked in Europe, now the British navy began a blockade of the major American harbors. England, which was not particularly enthusiastic about fighting its former colonists again, signed a peace treaty in 1814, almost simultaneous with Napoleon's defeat, which returned Anglo-American relations to their prewar status quo.

With peace finally reigning on both sides of the Atlantic Ocean, the tide of immigration to America was once again able to flow. And with vast new areas of the country opened up and ready for settlement, that tide would grow stronger in each succeeding year.

Chapter 6

The Flood Begins

New Yorkers reading the October 15, 1825, edition of the *Daily Advertiser* probably paid little attention to the following story:

> A vessel has arrived at this port with emigrants from Norway. The vessel is very small, measuring as we understand only about 360 Norwegian lasts, or forty-five American tons, and brought forty-six passengers, male and female, all bound to Ontario County [New York], where an agent, who came over some time since, purchased a tract of land. . . . [The] voyage [lasted] fourteen weeks; and all are in good health.[1]

The story did not give the name of the ship, which was the *Restoration*. The event, reported so undramatically, marks the coming of almost a million Norwegians to the United States in the nineteenth and twentieth centuries. In the history of Norwegian immigration to America, the *Restoration* is as important as the *Mayflower* was to English immigration two centuries earlier. The passengers on the *Restoration* were in the vanguard of millions of northern Europeans who added their bodies and their futures to the greatest human migration in history—the arrival of millions of immigrants in the United States in the nineteenth and early twentieth centuries.

In the one hundred years between 1815 and the outbreak of World War I, more than 20 million immigrants traveled across the Atlantic Ocean to America. And, just as the ocean does not move in a steady stream but in a series of waves, so too did immigration to America, but the series of waves became larger and larger. The first of these waves began shortly after Napoleon's defeat and continued until the American Civil War. In those years most of the immigrants came from the British Isles and northern Europe—from Germany, France, the Netherlands, Norway, and Sweden.

The United States was growing after the end of the War of 1812, and its growth went on for decades. Huge tracts of land, much of it acquired in the Louisiana Purchase, stood ready for settlement. A nationwide canal-building effort, highlighted by the opening of the Erie Canal in 1825 (through which an immigrant arriving in New York could travel, via the Great Lakes, as far west as Minnesota), made the new lands easily accessible. And new modes of travel—the steamship and the railroad —made getting there even easier.

Politically America became more receptive to new immigrants as well. Beginning in the 1820s voting requirements were gradually relaxed until, by the era of President Andrew Jackson, the so-called universal suffrage (the right of every white male citizen to vote) became the law of the land. Since immigrants did not have to wait long to become citizens, politicians, especially in the large eastern cities, began to see the newcomers not as aliens but as new voters.

America was ripe for settlers. But even so, what was it about America that so attracted the people of northern Europe that millions of them severed ancestral ties to come and make their fortunes in the New World? The interpretations vary widely. But Swedish immigrant Hans Mattson, writing after a long and distinguished career in his adopted country, probably summed up the feelings of his fellow immigrants best:

> Much has been said about the causes of emigration. These are numerous, but the chief cause I have found to be that people of the Old World are now being aroused to the fact that the social conditions of Europe, with its aristocracy and other privileges, are not founded on just principles, but that the way to success ought to be equally open for all, and determined, not by privileges of birth, but by in-

herent worth of man. And here in America is found a civilization which is, to a large extent, built on equality and the recognition of personal merit. This and the great natural resources of the country, the prospects of good wages, which the new continent affords, and in many cases religious liberty, draw the people of Europe, at any rate from Sweden, to this country.[2]

Mattson was quite eloquent in his reasons for the huge migration from Europe to America. Generalities like these often serve to describe broad trends. Yet immigration to America was almost always the result of a personal decision made, millions of times over, by individuals who were trying to fulfill their hopes and dreams. Often these people could not give a clear, logical reason for uprooting themselves from a way of life that had persisted for their kinsmen as far back as anyone could remember. The reasons for coming to America given by Gustaf Unonius, who left Sweden in 1841, typify those of the masses of people who also came, faced with the same dilemmas:

> I had within me the bitter discontent and sense of injustice one so often feels in youth towards one's position and the conditions under which one lives, when desires one feels to be just are not fulfilled as rapidly as one feels oneself is entitled to demand, when one is unjust both towards oneself and towards others, and every-

thing one believes to be in the way of one's
success in life—the government, the social
order, and society itself—gets the blame, and
one seems to see something rotten in it all. One
longs for a change—a desire for something,
one knows not what. . . .[3]

As anybody knows who has ever visited there,
Scandinavia is beautiful, parts of it breathtaking.
The large lakes of Sweden, the narrow fjords of
Norway, and the enormous brooding forests of both
countries are a refreshing delight to the eye. However, for people attempting to support themselves,
these scenic beauties are evidence of nature's stingi-
ness in Scandinavia. Three quarters of Norway is
barren, and only three percent of it could be cultivated in the nineteenth century. To land-starved
people, the stories of vast expanses of cheap, fertile
land in America seemed incredible. When the reality
sunk in that such lands actually did exist, the effect
was explosive. Over the course of a century, Norway
and Sweden each sent a million emigrants to
America—not particularly large numbers compared
to more populous countries like Germany and
Ireland. However, the Scandinavian countries had
such small populations (in 1850 Norway had 1.5
million people, Sweden 3.5 million) that the effect
was staggering. Some districts lost so many young
people to America that they had trouble functioning.
Most potential emigrants became convinced of
the truth of what they heard about America through

so-called America letters which were written by settlers in the New World to friends and relatives back home. In fact, it was just such a letter from Cleng Peerson—a Norwegian who, until his death in 1865, acted as a kind of pathfinder for Norwegian settlers—that attracted the *Restoration* group, or "sloopers" as they came to be called, to America. On December 20, 1824, Peerson wrote:

> I am letting you know that I have arrived, happy and well, in America. After a journey of six weeks, we reached New York. . . . We stayed there for five days and then took the steamboat *William Penn* for Albany, where we arrived in twenty-four hours. This was a distance of 150 miles. . . . The price for each of us was $2—and we also received free board.
>
> Later we went to Troy and then westward, through the great [Erie] canal, two hundred miles to Salina Salt Works, working our way. . . . I made my way overland to Geneva, where the land commissioner lives, to buy land for myself and for you as previously agreed. . . .
>
> I am already building a house, twelve by ten ells [an ell was roughly equivalent to a yard], which I hope to finish by New Year's day. We then expect winter to go on for a couple of months, and that will be a good time to haul wood from the forests. When I was in Rochester I bought a stove for $20, fully equipped with pans, pots for meat, a baking

oven, and other things—so we shall not need to build a fireplace. . . . I have five acres of land ready for sowing and planting in the spring. I have a cow in Farmington which cost me $10, and I have a few sheep.[4]

Chatty letters like these, full of the day-to-day details of settling in the New World were copied and recopied and carried from one part of Norway to another. In an age without television or radio, these words from afar served to inform people of what life would be like for them should they decide to try to make a new life for themselves in America. In mountainous Norway, where people tended to be isolated from each other and a knowledge of the outside world was difficult to come by, these letters had a dramatic effect.

There were no books or pamphlets to guide those who might be interested in leaving Norway— America letters served this purpose instead. Often the writers of letters back home were aware that their accounts of life in the New World would be passed from hand to hand, from village to village, and read by many of their interested countrymen. One such letter writer whose narratives were addressed to a wide audience was Gjert Hovland, a Norwegian who arrived in New York in 1831 and joined the slooper settlement in upstate New York. In a letter of 1835, Hovland gave this account of how he and his family were faring in America:

We are in the best of health, and . . . both my wife and I are exceedingly well satisfied. Our son attends the English school and talks English as well as the native born. Nothing has made me more happy and contented than that we left Norway and came to this country. We have gained more since our arrival here than I did during all the time I lived in Norway, and I have every prospect of earning a living here for myself and my family. . . .

I do not believe that any who suffer oppression and who must rear their children in poverty could do better than to come to America. But alas, many who want to come lack the means, and many others are so stupid as to believe that it is best to live in the country where they have grown up even if they have nothing but hard bread to satisfy their hunger. . . . We lived [in Norway] altogether too long. Nor have I talked with any immigrant in this country who wished to return.[5]

After only three years in the slooper settlement, Hovland set his sights for greener pastures—the vast expanses of land in the American West. Land there was much cheaper than in the East, which had been settled hundreds of years earlier. In an 1835 letter to Norway, Hovland described the trek that he anticipated making:

Six families of the Norwegians who had settled
in this place sold their farms last summer and
moved farther west in the country to a place
called Illinois. We and another Norwegian
family have also sold our farms and intend to
journey, this May, to that state, where land
can be bought at a better price, and where it
is easier to get started. . . . The United States
owns an untold amount of land, which is reserved by law at a set price for the one who
first buys it from the government. It is called
public land and is sold for $1.25 per acre. . . .
Whether native-born or foreign, a man is free
to do with it whatever he pleases.

This is a beautiful and fertile country.
Prosperity and contentment are almost everywhere. Practically everything needed can be
sown or planted here and grows splendidly,
producing a yield of many fold. . . .[6]

After settling in Illinois, Hovland became more
convinced than ever that America was the Promised
Land for his many fellow countrymen seeking a
better way of life for themselves. In a letter of 1838,
he described Illinois as a new Canaan, but he warned
those thinking of coming to America that their task
would not be easy:

I suppose that people are emigrating in great
numbers from Norway now, and every emigrant has a different attitude. . . . Anyone who

wants to make good here has to work, just as in all other places in the world. But here everything is better rewarded. This fact repels many people, though anyone with common sense ought to know that in time life rewards each as he deserves. Therefore, it seems to me all who take a notion to visit this country had better consider the matter carefully before they leave their homes, nor should they enter upon the venture frivolously or intoxicated by greed for material things.[7]

Letters like those that Hovland sent back to Norway encouraged thousands to emigrate to America. Even more influential was the first book written for prospective emigrants, *A True Account of America for the Information and Help of Peasant and Commoner,* written by Ole Rynning. Rynning came to America in 1837, and settled in Illinois, about seventy miles south of Chicago. He wrote his book while recovering from frostbite, and it was published in Norway in 1839. The effect was electrifying, as an eyewitness who lived in Rynning's hometown in Norway related:

For a time I believed that half the population of Snaasen had lost their senses. Nothing else was spoken of but the land that flows with milk and honey. Our minister, Ole Rynning's father, tried to stop the fever. Even from the pulpit he urged people to be discreet and described the hardships of the voyage and the cruelty of the American savage in the most forbidding colors. This was only pouring oil upon the fire.[8]

Like Norway, Sweden in the nineteenth century was ripe for large numbers of its population to emigrate, and America letters had their effect there also. As late as the middle of the nineteenth century, less than ten percent of the Swedish population worked in industry, while eighty percent earned their livelihood in agriculture in a land that could barely support them. Not surprisingly, when news of the fertile, cheap lands in America spread through the Swedish countryside, many people became caught up in "America fever."

Prior to 1840 very few America letters were sent to Swedish newspapers. Swedish law, until that time, prohibited emigration, and the few Swedes who had gone to America—mostly sailors who had jumped ship—were not anxious to let Swedish authorities know where they were. After the law was repealed, however, emigration began in earnest, including many Swedes of the middle class—students, merchants, civil servants, and intellectuals.

The America letters sent back to Sweden were much like their Norwegian counterparts. Many of them were printed in Swedish newspapers, and they soon became popular features. In an 1849 letter John Johansson gave his countrymen a glimpse of America as a paradise on earth:

No one need worry about my circumstances in America because I am living on God's noble and free soil, neither am I a slave under others. On the contrary, I am my own master, like the other creatures of God, I have now been on American soil for two and a half years and I have not been compelled to pay a penny for the privilege of living. Neither is my cap worn out from lifting it in the presence of gentlemen. There is no class distinction here between high and low, rich and poor, no make-believe, no "title sickness," or artificial ceremonies, but everything is quiet and peaceful and everybody lives in peace and prosperity. . . . The Americans do not have to scrape their effects together and sell them in order to pay heavy taxes to the crown and pay the salaries of officials.[9]

As the Norwegian and Swedish America letters demonstrate, the greatest attraction America held for the potential emigrant was the happy combination of cheap land, plentiful opportunities for work, and—most important—a young, democratic society, something almost unknown in the aristocracies of Europe. The French Revolution and the Napoleonic era had brought a taste of democratic ideas to Europe, but with Napoleon's downfall, the reforms made in the countries he conquered were revoked, and repressive regimes were once again installed.

Nowhere was this more evident than in the

German states, which supplied the greatest number
of emigrants to America in the early part of the
nineteenth century. By the outbreak of the Civil
War, Germans made up over thirty percent of
America's foreign-born population. German immi-
grants to America were farmers, craftsmen, intel-
lectuals, Protestants, Catholics, and Jews. Like
Scandinavia, Germany experienced its bouts of
America fever, which were inspired both by accounts
German immigrants to America sent back home and
by popular American novels by authors such as
James Fenimore Cooper, whose hero, Natty
Bumppo, roamed the American forests unhampered
by human laws.

The most influential of the German writers about
America was Gottfried Duden, whose book about
Missouri, which first appeared in 1829, went
through three editions. Duden's book made America
sound like the Garden of Eden, an image that must
have had a strong appeal to his hard-pressed readers.
In one section, after describing how he had set up
his own farm in Missouri, supporting himself and
his family very well on hunting and modest farming,
Duden wrote:

> After the household is once organized in this
> fashion and the first necessaries supplied, then
> the whole family lives carefree and happily
> without a single piece of ready money. . . . For
> taxes alone is ready money needed. But these
> taxes are so unimportant that one scarcely

thinks of them. Land acquired from the government is entirely tax free for the first five
years. . . .[10]

To live without taxes and without cares—that was
a vision of paradise. And to millions of northern
Europeans, whether German, Scandinavian, Dutch,
or French, that vision, repeated over and over again
by countrymen who had made the journey to
America, worked like a magnet, drawing them
across the Atlantic.

Chapter 7

Travel to the New Land

Once they made the decision to leave the Old World for America, most northern European immigrants had to undertake a double journey. First, they had to cross the Atlantic Ocean, and then, because most of them hoped to settle in the Midwest or the West, they had to make the overland journey to their new homes in America. Travel in the nineteenth century was somewhat faster and easier than it had been in the seventeenth and eighteenth centuries—especially after transatlantic steamships and transcontinental railroads were put into service—but the process of uprooting one's family and moving it to a new land was not without its difficulties and its dangers.

For most immigrants the trip to America began with months of preparation. Clothing for the journey had to be made, strong chests had to be built to hold the family's goods during the journey, and finally, the family members had to decide what goods they

would take with them and what would be left behind
or sold. Emigrants also needed time to prepare themselves psychologically for a journey that would re-
move them—perhaps forever—from the land of
their birth. "All through the winter darkness," one
Norwegian woman remembered, "I helped my
mother with the preparations. In the evening darkness my brother and I often sat and built air castles,
dreaming of what we should do when we got to
America."

When the time came for an emigrant to finally
leave for America—usually in the spring, when fair
weather offered the best chance for a smooth voyage
—the departure was commonly filled with tearful
farewells from relatives and friends they might never
see again. Departure for America was exciting for
most emigrants. Who wouldn't be excited at the
prospect of traveling thousands of miles to begin a
new life in a far-off land? But many left with mixed
emotions. Eric Norelius expressed the feelings of
thousands of emigrants in his account of his departure from Sweden, written in 1850:

> We put our little emigrant trunk in father's old
> cart, and with many tears and the breaking of
> tender heart-strings we bade farewell to our
> brothers and sisters. Mother went with us as far
> as the churchyard, so that she could say that
> she had followed us to the grave. . . . When we
> were a little past the farm called Bränslan, I
> turned to take a final look at our village,

Norrbäck, and I felt as if my heart was being
torn from my bosom. When we passed the dear
old church, my soul was again stirred to its
depths as I recalled that it was here I had been
baptized and confirmed and had taken part in
the worship, and now I would most likely never
see it again. . . .[1]

The trip to a seaport from which to sail for
America could be difficult, especially if the distance
emigrants had to travel was great. That was the case
for most Germans who came to America prior to
the Civil War. Most of these emigrants came from
southern Germany. The nearest port from which
they could take a ship to America was Havre,
France, some four hundred miles from their homelands. A French writer who witnessed the mass
German exodus to America in the 1840s wrote an
account of the difficult conditions emigrants from
Bavaria had to contend with in reaching Havre:

It is a lamentable sight when you are travelling
in the spring or autumn on the Strasburg road,
to see the long files of carts that meet you every
mile, carrying the whole property of the poor
wretches, who are about to cross the Atlantic
on the faith of a lying prospectus. There they
go slowly along; their miserable tumbrils
[wagons]—drawn by such starved, drooping
beasts, that your only wonder is, how they can
possibly hope to reach Havre alive—piled with
the scanty boxes containing their few effects,

and on top of all the women and children, the sick and bedridden, and all who are too exhausted with the journey to walk. One might take it for a convoy of wounded, the relics of a battlefield, but for the rows of little white heads peeping from beneath the ragged hood.[2]

Ship travel to America for the immigrant tended to be haphazard over the first half of the nineteenth century, and there were no regulations that governed shipboard conditions. Most of the ships that carried immigrants took them on as a sideline; their major function was carrying American goods to Europe and European goods back to America. People who wanted to sail to America had to take their chances in selecting a ship for the voyage because conditions varied greatly from ship to ship. Most immigrants, the majority of whom were simple farmers, were no match for the hustlers and the sharpies who infested the docks, waiting to prey on them. An article published in 1850 condemned these "land sharks":

There is to be found continually a set of men, who have been forced to quit Germany, and with the purpose of going to America or who can say by what other chance have got to this place, where they now seek to keep up their life by making themselves busy with the emigrants. In all our travels in different countries, we have never met with more miserable men, a class more destitute of morality, than these land sharks, who lie in wait for these thus come by

thousands from Germany, thrust themselves
upon them as countrymen and friends . . .
detain their victims, plunder them, and abuse
their inexperience in the most shameful
way. . . .[3]

Until the 1850s the Atlantic crossing was made
in sailing ships that took about two months to get
from Europe to America. For those few immigrants
who could afford to travel first class, the trip could
be comfortable, even luxurious. But luxury travel
arrangements were the exception rather than the
rule, and most immigrants made the trip under
difficult conditions. Jan Bosman, a Dutch tailor, left
an account of what a typical voyage was like—a
description of his own trip to America in 1856:

We left on our journey to America, in the
Revenue, sailing from Rotterdam. This was a
small American ship, not equipped to transport
human beings. But they hastily erected some
rude shelters, in which we were to sleep. . . .
Our quarters were hardly fit for passengers.
Such was the stench below deck, that my wife's
first thought was that she could not stand it.
This was no easy voyage with two children, the
oldest 22 months, the youngest 4 months. But
the Lord provided.[4]

Despite the poor conditions on board ship,
Bosman was relieved when, after the *Revenue* had
left port, it met with fair weather and smooth

sailing. Then, midway through the voyage, storms
struck the small ship, tossing it to and fro, making
the passengers' lives miserable. Bosman continued
to describe the voyage:

> Our food was of meager quality. Dinner was
> best, at other times we were served hard ship
> biscuit. This was so hard that we had to ration
> hot water with which to soak it so that we could
> eat it, for water was not plentiful on board our
> ship. In this way we sailed [into] New York
> [Harbor].
>
> Then we were glad and filled with joy; we
> promised ourselves a good meal as soon as we
> set foot on land. Our boxes and trunks were
> transferred to a flatboat. When these boxes
> were put on shore we were permitted to enter
> Castle Garden [where immigrants were met by
> American officials]. We were asked various
> questions: How old we were; our place of
> origin; how much money we carried; and about
> other matters.
>
> A touching incident happened here. An aged
> man, from our part of Gelderland, who traveled
> with us and had lost much strength because of
> the poor food was brought from the flatboat
> into Castle Garden supported by two men. He
> died at Castle Garden.[5]

The quality of a transatlantic voyage often depended upon the captain of the ship—his attitude
toward the emigrants and his leadership of his crew

determined how passengers were treated. While crossings could be quite pleasant, more often than not, well-intentioned immigrants found themselves trapped on board ship for weeks or months, their surroundings uncomfortable or worse, their rations meager, and their lives endangered. An 1853 account, written by a Norwegian immigrant to America, describes just how bad the crossings could be:

> The crossing was terrible. Three days after we had left land, we had a frightful storm, and during the night we lost the mainmast and the foremast, so that later we had to get along by means of jury-rigged masts and sails. Many of the berths on the lower deck collapsed, and water poured down through the hatchways so that coffers, trunks, sacks, and all kinds of loose objects floated around in the water. . . . That many provisions were spoilt and clothes and the like damaged by the water is easy to understand. This storm lasted two days and two nights, and during this time we had to go both hungry and thirsty, since we could not manage to prepare anything. . . . [and] could not get any fresh water either.[6]

The Norwegian immigrant had taken passage on this particular ship because of a brochure the company that owned the ship had circulated in his home village in Norway. The brochure promised comfortable berths, ample food and water, and a smooth passage. After being on board ship for a while, though, the dismayed passengers found that:

> In the galley there was a large stove; but as there were always a lot of people who wanted to cook, the only law that prevailed here was club law. The strongest and most aggressive could always, although with difficulty, get something cooked, while the weaker and more timid got nothing or had to content themselves with being the last in line, at the risk of having their pots, with half-cooked food, thrown off the fire when the stronger were pleased to come back.
>
> Fights and quarrels were daily occurrences, and the company had done nothing to make sure that everybody was treated justly and the promises that had been made were kept. In Christiania we were promised all sorts of things —for instance, that the food would be excellent. With regard to this, let me give you just one small illustration of the way these promises were kept. Every Saturday we got our provisions; they consisted of six or seven biscuits, about three eighths of a pound of brown sugar, a little wheat flour, some rice and groats, and ten pounds of beef; the meat was to last for the whole passage, but most of it was bone. . . .
>
> At our departure we were promised a

sufficient amount of fresh water, but we got so
little that we had to be satisfied with making a
small cup of tea in the morning and cooking a
little porridge later in the day. As for getting
water to quench our thirst, that was out of the
question. We could not make any broth with
the meat we had been given. . . .[7]

Despite the bad conditions on board ship and
despite the fact that the company had misled immigrants about what to expect, this immigrant, like so
many others, remained undaunted. Once he arrived
in America, he found that the new land more than
lived up to his expectations. Nevertheless, the
Atlantic crossing was a poor introduction to
America. "From the knowledge I have of America
now," the young Norwegian concluded, "I think I
shall never suffer such want anywhere as I did on
board the ship, where we were so starved and thirsty
that I thought I should never set foot on land again.
God be praised. . . ."[8]

The northern European immigrants came in such
large numbers that some parts of America took on
a special ethnic character. Wisconsin's German
flavor and Minnesota's Scandinavian tone still exist
to remind us that these states were havens to millions
of immigrants seeking a new home in the nineteenth
century. Weakened by the long Atlantic crossing,
most immigrants landed in America confused and
bewildered by the new environment they en-

countered. Yet, having survived run-ins with land sharks on one side of the ocean, most of them now had to deal with another predator, the emigrant entrapper—entrepreneurs who made their livelihood by preying on new immigrants. The commissioners of emigration of New York investigated the unscrupulous practices of the emigrant entrappers as a prelude to cleaning up the abuse. What they uncovered was a gauntlet of dockside swindlers who thought nothing of stripping an immigrant of the meager funds he or she had managed to scrape together to make a new start in America. Tobias Boudinot, a New York City police captain, testified about what new arrivals had to contend with:

> Many of the steamboats that land emigrants . . . land at the docks in the Third Ward. They are immediately visited by runners from the emigrant boarding houses, backed by bullies to assist in soliciting passengers to go to the different houses. As the emigrant attempts to take his luggage from on board the boat, the runner will endeavor to get it from him and by force, unless there is sufficient police to protect him, representing that they will keep them at sixpence sterling for each meal and sixpence sterling for lodging, and no charge for cartage or storage of luggage. When the emigrant comes to pay his bill, he is never able to get off at the contract price, but is compelled to

pay from three shillings to fifty cents for each
meal and lodging, one dollar and fifty cents for
cartage . . . and other things in proportion.[9]

The problem of emigrant entrapment became so
severe, in fact, that a magazine article on the subject
offered the following tongue-in-cheek advice to
would-be immigrants:

> The best way to avoid being plundered in New
> York is to arrive in the happy condition of
> having nothing to lose. Poverty is the best of
> all safeguards against knavery. Disembarking
> penniless, unwell, and disconsolate, the immi-
> grant passes into the hands of a very different
> class of persons from those described (the
> entrappers)—namely, the commissioners of
> emigration, whose deeds of charity and mercy
> are beyond all praise.[10]

Between the long, difficult journey from their
home villages to the nearest transatlantic port, the
schemes of land sharks, the often intolerable conditions found on board ship, and the voracity of
emigrant entrappers in America once the new land
had been reached, immigrating to America was no
easy task. Yet despite such difficulties, millions of
northern Europeans made the journey. Each had his
or her story to tell. And ultimately, each made
his or her contribution to life in the new land—to
America.

Chapter 8

Settling on the Frontier

Most of the northern Europeans who immigrated to pre–Civil War America were farmers. Huge amounts of virgin land awaited the plow in America—but, unlike the seventeenth and eighteenth centuries, when fertile land was available near the major eastern seaports, in the nineteenth century unsettled land was to be had only in the West. For these settlers, then, coming to find their fortunes in America meant traveling thousands of miles inland, to farm sites in Minnesota or Wisconsin, Texas or Kansas, or even farther west, to California and Oregon.

Between 1835 and 1860 the United States underwent a huge expansion in size, guided by the claim of a "Manifest Destiny," that is, Americans had the right and the duty to incorporate all of North America into the Union. Congress welcomed Texas into the Union in 1845 and declared war on Mexico in 1846. This resulted in the annexation of California and the present-day southwestern states, together with a good-sized Mexican population. The government also settled a long-standing border dispute with England over the Oregon Territory, which gave the United States government clear title to what is now the Pacific Northwest. With the discovery of gold in California in 1848—and the resultant gold rush that brought thousands of people to the West Coast, America, for the first time, stretched "from sea to shining sea."

Land was cheap and plentiful in the West—usually at the expense of the local Indian tribes from whom it was taken—and newly built canals and railroads made it easy for newcomers to get there. In 1862 Congress passed the Homestead Act in an effort to attract more people to the West. The act gave 160 acres of federally owned land to any settler who lived on the land for five years and farmed it. To land-starved Europeans, the prospect of abundant, cheap, arable land available at a small cost or —unbelievably—for free made America an irresistible attraction.

There were various routes to the West that a newly arrived immigrant could take, but the most popular one, until the railroads were built, was by boat up the Hudson River, through the Erie Canal, and then to the Great Lakes. By connecting the Atlantic Ocean and the Great Lakes, the Erie Canal allowed newcomers to reach the fertile Midwest easily, and it permitted produce and raw materials from the Midwest to reach important markets in the East. Jacob Schramm, a German immigrant who traveled through the canal in 1836 on his way to Indiana, left an account of what a journey on the Erie Canal was like:

We arranged for the trip to Buffalo in a canal-boat: sleeping quarters, and meals with the captain, 8 dollars each. This is a distance of 360 English miles . . . and the trip lasted 7 days. The boats were suitably fitted up. There are three cabins: a small one where the women passengers sleep; a second, with benches, which at night are put together and made into beds for the men; and a third where meals are served. Next to the dining room is the kitchen, where the sailors and the cook have their quarters. In the middle is the large space for goods. The boats are not very large, about 50 feet long and 10 wide, with the lower deck just high enough so a man can stand upright; nevertheless everything is surprisingly well managed. . . .

The boat is drawn by horses, usually in relays of two, and day and night they keep up a sharp pace. The canal is only 4 or 5 feet deep, and of course the boats are built in accordance. For the most part they are the property of companies in New York or Albany, or other cities along the way, and have connections at all the landings. There are companies

that have 300 such boats, which continually
take goods and people to the western states,
and bring produce to the eastern states.[1]

Schramm, like most other immigrants who
traveled along the Erie Canal, was overwhelmed by
the vastness of America's interior and by the canal
itself. In another section of his narrative, he
described the intricate system of locks, by which the
canalboats traversed the interior of New York State:

> The first day we passed many locks, and that
> delayed the trip. The canal is for the most part
> laid out where the country is flattest, but as all
> the hills cannot be avoided, locks have to be
> built, which must cost frightful sums. There
> are perhaps 200 between Albany and Buffalo
> [the two ends of the canal]. At the entrance
> into one of these locks, built from quarried
> stone, there is a pair of gates, which is closed
> when the boat is once inside. The upper section
> of the canal, perhaps 10 or 15 feet higher, is
> held by another gate, which is closed while one
> is going through the lower gate, and then
> opened as soon as the lower one is closed. As
> the water comes rushing through the gate of
> the lock, the water and the boat at the closed
> door are lifted, rising to the height of the upper
> level. This process is repeated until one is up
> the hill. . . .[2]

The trip westward gave most immigrants their first look at America and its customs. More important, because the newcomers traveled through lands that had been settled for some time, they saw what could be done to develop thriving farms and towns. This exposure often proved invaluable, for once the immigrants reached their destinations, they often found that conditions weren't as they had been advertised in the America letters they had read back home in Europe. An anonymous Swedish immigrant, writing home in the 1850s, sadly reported:

> We often find that he who relates that he owns a saw-mill only owns a saw and a saw-buck, and he who describes the beautiful carriage he owns, is the owner of a wheelbarrow for which himself serves as the locomotive.[3]

Gloomy reports such as these were reprinted in newspapers in Europe, where they received wide circulation. Alarmed at the massive loss of population to America, many preachers and government officials used these reports to discourage emigration. Often, frightening details were added to these accounts: Prospective emigrants were told that wild beasts would devour them on the American frontier, that savage Indians would scalp them, or that they would be sold into slavery. But these horror stories had little effect. Conditions in Europe were so unpromising and the lure of America was so great that the flow of emigrants continued unabated.

In spite of the crude conditions many emigrants encountered when they first arrived on the frontier, most were able to see in the unspoiled land possibilities for the future. Rev. Olof Olsson, writing from his settlement in Kansas in the 1860s, had little patience with his fellow Swedes who complained about the hardships of American life. Instead, he looked to the rewards that hard work would bring to his new community and his new land:

> You should see our settlement out here. It is a beautiful sight. Prairie and still more prairie. Here and there a line of green trees on both sides of the winding Smokey Hill River or in the small valleys where water seeks an outlet. . . . Many who come, overwhelmed by this dreary prairie, do not take time to dig a hole in order to observe the rich soil, which nourishes the luxuriant grass. They turn back immediately, or devote themselves to idle sorrow. The only thing they do is write long lamentations to Sweden. . . . It has been wonderful this summer to see the large seeded fields, which a few years ago belonged to the buffalo and Indians. The crop in Kansas has really been excellent this year, although our settlement has not profited much from it, since all of us have just arrived. . . .
>
> We do not dig gold with pocket knives, we do not expect to become bountifully rich in a few days or in a few years, but what we aim

at is to own our own homes, where each one has his own property, which with God's blessings will provide him with the sustenance which he and his family need. . . . The advantage which America offers is not to make everyone rich at once without toil and trouble, but the advantage is that the poor, who will and are able to work, secure a large piece of good land almost without cost, that they can work up little by little. . . .[4]

Olsson was correct in his judgment that to succeed in building up a small farm on the frontier required a good deal of hard work. Laborsaving machinery was not introduced on a large scale until after the Civil War, and even with the new machines such as threshers and reapers, farm life remained hard. Chrysostom Adrian Verwyst, who came to Wisconsin from Holland when he was seven years old, left behind an accurate description of what farming on the frontier was like:

Farming in those days on land full of stumps and roots was conducted in very primitive fashion. When a man had succeeded in cutting down the trees and chopping them into logs of fourteen to sixteen feet in length, he had to pile them up. This was a laborious task, especially if he had no oxen or horses. I remember how, when I was a lad of about thirteen, we had to work with might and main to roll up the heavy logs into piles to burn. . . . When the difficult task of burning the logs and brush had been accomplished, we cultivated the land thus wrested from the primitive forest.

For the first two years we had no oxen and so were compelled to plow with heavy grub hoes. Oftentimes our wrists would ache from digging and working in the hard, rooty ground. We could hoe a great number of hills in which to plant potatoes and corn. When the plants appeared above ground it was necessary to hoe them again to kill the weeds and get the crops to grow. . . . It was hard slavish work throughout the entire year. There were no mowing machines, and I remember seeing father cut our grain with a sickle, such as was used 4,000 years ago. . . . Haymaking was carried on much as it had been in Old Testament times. Heat, fatigue, and sweat were expended lavishly in procuring food for the stock.[5]

Because he came to Wisconsin at such a young age, Verwyst saw his father's dream—the product of all his family's sweat and labor—become a reality. Little by little, the wilderness gave way to civilization, and Verwyst was a witness to the process:

In spite of the want of modern machinery, however, the farms grew in size and value year by year. First, five to ten acres of stumpy and rooty land, a small log house with wooden chimney and floor made of hewn logs or rough boards, a small stable for the cattle, a pigpen,

and a henhouse—such were the rude begin-
nings of farm life in those days. However,
things began gradually to change for the better.
Frame house and barn took the place of the
old log buildings; horses replaced the slow,
patient oxen; the roads became more fit for
travel; board fences replaced those made of
rails; thus primitive Wisconsin developed into
one of the most prosperous states in the Union.
This transformation was largely wrought by the
strong arm and tireless industry of the now-
sometimes-despised foreigner.[6]

Most immigrants retained a strong sense of their
own ethnic identities, which often lasted down
through several generations, and they were conscious
of the ethnic origins of others. In the following
account, written by a Norwegian immigrant named
Johan Gasmann, it is evident that it seemed only
natural to identify people by their country of origin:

As I stepped ashore from the steamboat, I met
a Dane by the name of Fribert and a Swede
named Petersson. The first I already knew by
name, and for his later courtesy, I owe him
thanks. . . . I lodged that night in a little white-
painted inn which bore the sign "Lafayette,"
the owner of which was a Frenchman. The man
had not forgotten his French courtesy, and
when I exchanged a few French words with
him, he became quite spirited. The lodging was
very good and quite cheap. For bed and board,

a bottle of Bavarian ale, tobacco and a pipe, I
paid in all eighteen cents. As arranged, Mr.
Fribert, Mr. Petersson and his daughter . . .
and I set out in the morning in a four-wheeled
wagon with two horses, which we hired from
an Irishman. . . .[7]

Gasmann was hardly surprised to encounter
people with five different ethnic backgrounds; in
America, it was what he had come to expect. But
even though most immigrants, like Gasmann, retained a strong sense of their country of origin and
were concerned about preserving their native
languages and Old World traditions, they adapted
quickly to the American style of the time. In fact,
reading the letters written home by immigrants from
different countries, as well as those of other Americans, it is evident that most settlers on the frontier
shared the same outlook and interests. They were
concerned with the same things: land values, the
extension of the railroad into their areas, crops, and
—especially for those on the very edge of the
frontier—Indian attack.

America's expansionist plunge westward inevitably aggravated a problem that had existed since
the first discovery of the New World by Europeans:
the clash of cultures and economic interests between
whites and native Americans. White settlers ruthlessly swept the Indians aside whenever the Indians
got in their way. When it was convenient to acknowledge native American titles to their land, whites

recognized them. When Indian claims frustrated the whites' desires, however, they were ignored.

One of the first large-scale invasions of settlers in the lands west of the Mississippi River took place in Wisconsin. The disregard of native American rights there led to a series of uprisings that culminated in the capture of the Sauk leader, Black Hawk, in 1832. A proud, fighting warrior, Black Hawk summarized for generations to come the tragedy that befell native Americans at the hands of the white settlers. En route to an army stockade following his capture, Black Hawk looked back on his long war with the whites:

> I surveyed the country that had cost us so much trouble, anxiety and blood, and that now caused me to be a prisoner of war. I reflected upon the ingratitude of the whites, when I saw their fine houses, rich harvests, and every thing desirable around them; and recollected that all this land had been ours, for which me and my people had never received a dollar, and that the whites were not satisfied until they took our village and our grave-yards from us. . . . [8]

Black Hawk and the other native American leaders could not hold back the tide of settlement into the fertile western lands. The invasion of Indian country accelerated as news of the rich lands west of the Mississippi filtered back to the East and Europe. During the 1850s the valley of the Minnesota River, which until then had almost no permanent white settlers, increased its population tenfold. By 1861, there were 18,000 Germans and 12,000 Scandinavians living in the valley.

The center of German settlement in the valley was New Ulm. Unlike most western settlements, which were haphazard and initiated by individual effort, New Ulm was part of an organized venture aimed at resettling German immigrants in the West. The development of New Ulm was orderly and regulated: The town was first surveyed, then land was cleared, and finally, homes were built. As German immigrants began arriving by steamboat, they built stores, breweries, schools, churches, libraries, and other institutions essential to a settled society.

As the Minnesota Valley filled up with white settlers and farms began encroaching on their hunting grounds, the local Sioux Indians became apprehensive. They were aware of what had happened farther to the east, where white settlers pushed native Americans off their land. With the reduction of army troops on the frontier as a result of the outbreak of the Civil War, the Sioux, under the leadership of their chief, Little Crow, saw their chance to drive the whites out. The Minnesota Valley was convulsed by a series of bloody attacks. Of the 200 houses in New Ulm, for example, nearly 150 were burned to the ground. The following account describes Indian uprisings that exacted a heavy toll:

Northern European immigrants retained a strong sense of their country of origin, but adapted quickly to the American style of the time. Fourth of July festivities, 1911. Hedlund Family, St. Paul, Minnesota. (Photo by James Pavlicek. Courtesy of the Minnesota Historical Society.)

The first group of Germans to emigrate to William Penn's Proprietorship were the Mennonites, who were looking for religious freedom. Mennonites. Meeting House Service. (Photo by Elmer Clifton. Courtesy of the New York Public Library Picture Collection.)

The Amish, too, wished to worship in their own way and still preserve many seventeenth-century German and Swiss traditions, including dress styles and the horse and buggy. Amish schoolchildren racing past teacher's carriage parked in yard of a one-room schoolhouse in eastern Lancaster County, Pennsylvania, 1979. (Courtesy of Wide World Photos.)

German immigrant Thomas Nast became known as the Father of the American Political Cartoon. But he may be best remembered for his pictorial creation of Santa Claus. "Merry Christmas to all, and to all a good-night." (Thomas Nast, *Christmas Drawings for the Human Race* [1890].)

Prior to World War II, the German-American Bund tried to get German-Americans to become "race-conscious." The Bund failed to interest many immigrants in Nazi ideology. Police Line Holds Crowd at Bund Rally in New York, February 20, 1939. (Courtesy of Wide World Photos.)

Refugee intellectuals from Germany during the 1930s had a tremendous influence on American culture. Taking the oath of citizenship, Trenton, New Jersey, October 1, 1940. *From left to right:* Helene Dukas, Secretary to Einstein, Professor Albert Einstein, and his daughter, Margot. (Photo courtesy of Wide World Photos.)

One of the early explorers in the New World, Frenchman Jacques Cartier sailed
the length of the St. Lawrence River but failed to found a colony. *Voyage of J.
Cartier in Canada, July 3, 1534.* (Lithograph by David from painting by Gadin.
Courtesy of The New-York Historical Society.)

The Sauk leader Black Hawk was finally taken prisoner after fighting the white settlers' invasion of Wisconsin. "I reflected upon the ingratitude of the whites . . . and recollected that all this land had been ours, for which me and my people had never received a dollar." Black Hawk *(third from left),* his sons, and followers in chains, Jefferson Barracks, 1832. (Pencil drawing by George Catlin from *Souvenir of the North American Indian,* London, 1850. Courtesy of Rare Book Collection, the New York Public Library.)

Hudson did not find a shorter route to Asia, but a majestic new river in North America. It still bears his name. *Landing of Hendrik Hudson.* (From the original picture by R. W. Weir. Courtesy of Allusion Archive.)

Prior to the opening of Ellis Island, Castle Garden, at the foot of Manhattan, served as the receiving station for immigrants. It had once been a fort and then a theater. "Castle Garden." (Lithograph from *100 Views of New York and Environs,* published by Charles Magnus. Courtesy of the Museum of the City of New York.)

By connecting the Atlantic Ocean and the Great Lakes, the Erie Canal allowed newcomers to reach the Midwest easily. *View on the Erie Canal,* 1830–32. (Watercolor drawing by J. W. Hill. Courtesy of the New York Public Library.)

Many of the early French Protestant immigrants were skilled craftsmen. Workers, such as this one making high-grade tapestries in New York City in 1920, earned wealth and influence in the U.S. (Photo by Lewis Hine. Courtesy of the New York Public Library.)

Land was cheap and plentiful in the West, and newly built railroads made it easy to get there. *Across the Continent, Westward the Course of Empire Takes Its Way.* New York, 1868. (Lithograph by Currier & Ives. Courtesy of The New-York Historical Society.)

Augustus Francis Sherman was an official at the Ellis Island Immigrant Station around the turn of the century. He was also an amateur photographer. He recorded on film the arrival of immigrants, who were often in colorful national dress. His photographs are collected at The Statue of Liberty National Monument and are reprinted here by courtesy of The National Park Service.

Johanna Dÿkhoff, 40, an immigrant from Holland with 11 children via the *Noordam*, May 12, 1908, on the way to Loretta, Minnesota.

Two Dutch immigrants.

Finnish immigrant family.

Two Swedish immigrants.

Most immigrants made the ocean voyage to the United States under difficult conditions. Steerage Deck of the S.S. *Pennland*, Red Star Line, 1893. (Photo by Byron. Courtesy of the Museum of the City of New York.)

Danish-born journalist and photographer Jacob Riis provided Americans with their
first real look at the conditions poor people and immigrants had to grapple with in
American cities at the end of the nineteenth century. Two Ragamuffins: "Didn't
live nowhere." (Photo by Jacob A. Riis. Courtesy of the Museum of the City of
New York.)

Photographer Lewis Hine also recorded the experience of poor people in cities in the early twentieth century. Backyard playground used by workers' children, Boston, 1912. (Courtesy of the New York Public Library.)

I will now describe everything to you as thoroughly as I am able, and as far as my heart, which is trembling with fear, will allow me. . . . The Indians have begun attacking the farmers. They have already killed a great many people, and many are mutilated in the cruelest manner. Tomahawks and knives have already claimed many victims. Children, less able to defend themselves, are usually burned alive or hanged in the trees, and destruction moves from house to house. The Indians burn everything on their way—houses, hay, grain, and so on. I believe that even if I described the horror in the strongest possible language, my description would fall short of reality. . . . These troubles have now lasted for about two weeks, and every day larger numbers of settlers come into St. Peter [Minnesota] to protect their lives from the raging Indians. They crowd themselves together in large stone houses for protection, and the misery is so great that imagination could not depict it in darker colors. A few persons arrive almost naked, others wounded by bullets or other weapons, and some with their hands and feet burned off. May I never again have to see such terrible sights! Those who have enough money to move on travel farther down in the country, but it is not safe where they go, for the whole country is in a state of turmoil and the Indians are found almost everywhere.[9]

In spite of the casualties they inflicted, the native Americans could not hope to drive the white settlers from their lands. They were vastly outnumbered by the whites, who also possessed weapons that were far superior to those available to the Indians. The Sioux uprising in the Minnesota Valley—and all the others that followed it—were minor roadblocks to the advancing line of settlement on the frontier. Within a few months of the Sioux uprising, for example, New Ulm and other ravaged settlements were completely rebuilt, and immigration to the West continued.

Chapter 9

Settling in the Cities

While most of the northern European immigrants who came to America prior to the Civil War were farmers, many city dwellers came to the new land as well. These newcomers were attracted to the bustling urban centers of the New World, and as a result, American cities expanded enormously. New York, for example, which had a population of only sixty thousand in 1800, grew to a city of more than one million people by 1860. As urban settlers moved west, they helped to change cities like St. Louis, Chicago, and Cincinnati from minor frontier outposts to major metropolitan centers. For a time St. Louis doubled its population every nine years; Cincinnati every seven years.

As with immigrants who came to America to farm, urban immigrants were drawn to the rapidly growing cities by the promise of economic improvement. The Old World looked on the New as a land

105

of abundance, a magical place where "the streets were paved with gold." And to many northern European newcomers, America indeed lived up to that promise. Some, however, were appalled by what they saw as American wastefulness. Edward Bok, a Dutch immigrant who came to the United States as a boy of six and went on to become famous as the editor of the *Ladies' Home Journal,* described in his memoirs how different life in the New World was from life in his native Holland:

I had been taught in my home across the sea that thrift was one of the fundamentals in a successful life. My family had come from a land (the Netherlands) noted for its thrift; but we had been in the United States only a few days before the realization came home strongly to my father and mother that they had brought their children to a land of waste.

Where the Dutchman saved, the American wasted. There was waste, and the most prodigal waste, on every hand. In every street-car and on every ferry-boat the floors and seats were littered with newspapers that had been read and thrown away or left behind. If I went to a grocery stores to buy a peck of potatoes, and a potato rolled off the heaping measure, the grocery-man, instead of picking it up, kicked it into the gutter for the wheels of his wagon to run over. The butcher's waste filled my mother's soul with dismay. If I bought a scuttle of coal at the corner grocery, the coal that missed the scuttle [a bucket], instead of being shovelled up and put back into the bin, was swept into the street. My young eyes quickly saw this; in the evening I gathered up the coal thus swept away, and during the course of a week, I collected a scuttleful. . . .[1]

Bok's account, based on recollections of his boyhood in the 1870s, ignores another consequence of mass immigration to the cities—the growth of the urban slum, beginning in the 1840s. Municipal services we take for granted—a safe water supply, police and fire protection, public transportation, and garbage collection—either were not provided or were primitive. With the extra demands made by expanding populations, these services often broke down. Housing was in short supply, and overcrowding was common—especially in poor immigrant neighborhoods. Ironically, the growth of the slums was viewed as a sign of material progress in the young industrial age because the increased population provided much of the labor for industry. The immigrants in the poor neighborhoods, however, often paid a high price:

The . . . Ward was densely crowded with working classes . . . [and] showed a high rate of sickness and mortality, owing to the overcrowded and ill-ventilated dwellings. . . .

The tenants are all Germans. . . . They are exceedingly filthy in person and their bedclothes are as dirty as the floors they walk on. Their food is of the poorest quality, and their feet and hands, doubtless their whole bodies are suffering from what they call rheumatism, but which in reality is a prostrate nervous system, the result of foul air and inadequate supply of nutritious food. . . . Not one decent sleeping apartment can be found on the entire premises and not one stove properly arranged. . . . The rooms are 6 by 10 feet. The inhabitants lead a miserable existence, and their children wilt and die in their infancy.[2]

Harsh as life could be in the cities, the immigrant's attitude toward the new country was generally not one of despair, but of accomplishment. The immigrants had made a hard and dangerous voyage to America. If poverty welcomed them on their arrival, at least it was no worse than the poverty they had left behind in Germany, Holland, or Scandinavia. And in America, unlike Europe, an immigrant could quickly improve his economic condition through hard work and diligence.

Typical of the experiences of many immigrants was that of Jacob Lanzit, who arrived in America from Austria in 1858 and set out to make his way in the New World. After arriving in New York, Lanzit wrote that it was "altogether too big to find anyone. This noise, this tumult, rattling traffic, drove me out of my mind."[3] Lanzit bought a railroad ticket for Chicago, twelve hundred miles inland, and recorded in his diary his financial progress over the next year:

> [In Chicago] I had myself taken to a German hotel, Hotel Meisner, [run by] a very decent man. Oh, how the blood stopped in my veins, not having spoken a word to anyone during the whole journey! I realized that I lack the English language. . . .
>
> Thurs [Sept.] the thirtieth. I went, recommended by an offis, to an innkeeper who needs a porter, who is supposed to pay board and $2 per week. I, for one, would be satisfied, but he believes that I am too good for this kind of work. He said, however, I should inquire tomorrow again. . . .
>
> Octob. 1. No chance of getting job with the innkeeper. I went to several tobacco dealers; perhaps they can use me in the factories. . . .
>
> Saturday, October 2nd. As I see, there is nothing to this either. I went from store to store and offered my services. No one would give me even an indefinite answer; they all said everything was taken.
>
> Serious, bad, very bad. To be sure, I still have enough to live on for ten to twelve months, but the question is, what then, perhaps use my pistols?[4]

Fortunately, a cigar manufacturer set Lanzit up with a tobacco stand at a local hotel, which he ran profitably until the hotel went out of business six months later. Seeking a better economic climate, he set out by railroad for the East. In Albany, New York, on January 5, 1859, Lanzit

> decided to learn a profession; that is, to learn either to make cigars or to sew on Singer's machine. I decided on the latter and began in earnest. Tuition $3. I will probably have to learn for five or six weeks. However, I can make a living. It is hard work, to be sure, but I am now in America; that means working. By chance I got into a factory after ten days' training, though for small wages.
>
> February 20. Still in the same factory with higher wages. By the end of February our factory closed down. I went around for three weeks without work. . . . I bought a machine [of my own] for $40 and went without eating. . . .
>
> All at once I advertised in the paper and was hired by a lining maker for $9 a week. . . .[5]

In just six months Jacob Lanzit had gone from a penniless unskilled immigrant to a self-employed sewing machine operator—an achievement many immigrants were able to equal. In the closing months of Lanzit's diary of his first year in America, he set forth, plainly and simply, "the American Dream":

> July and August. I worked industriously all the time. Finally I saved something, and on

> August 1, I deposited $20 in the bank, and
> on the same day I [met] a girl named M [is] s
> Rachel Max. That was on Monday. The fol-
> lowing Sunday I went out with her for the first
> time, to Central Parc [sic]. We love each other
> to a most extraordinary degree.
>
> Sunday, August 14. I bought a Singer's
> machine and traded in my machine, and Mon-
> day, August 15, I entered into partnership
> with a certain Liwey and, God willing, we
> will do well.[6]

What Lanzit describes in this entry is the ful-
fillment of the promise of America, which made it
such a different place from Europe. In America a
newcomer could advance quickly. If New York
wasn't to his or her liking, the immigrant could go
to Chicago, or St. Louis, or San Francisco. And if
the cities failed to satisfy, there was always the vast
American interior, dotted with farming communities. Social mobility like this was unknown in Europe. There, by and large, a person was forced by
the traditions of European society to work as his
or her parents had worked, from generation to
generation.

Still, Jacob Lanzit was luckier than most immigrants. Many northern European immigrants depended on relatives already in America or, more
often, immigrant self-help societies to aid them in
settling in the New World. As a result certain pat-
terns began to develop in the ways immigrants came

to America, in the cities they tended to settle in, and even in the type of business they were attracted to.

One nineteenth-century observer noted the extraordinary attraction that the grocery business seemed to hold for German immigrants. He discovered a long chain of German grocers, stretching from the Old World to the New; and this unbroken chain, the observer found, served to help new immigrants establish themselves in America:

> The grocer [for whom the newly arrived immigrant works] is always a German countryman. Before these people came to New York the Americans must have run these businesses themselves. But for a long time it has been quite different; these Germans have a monopoly on groceries. And there are few such Germans who in their lifetime have not been grocers, or, at least expected to be.
>
> The [immigrant] German strips off the marks of foreignness in a short time. After a single year he is no longer green, and no one can discern how short a time he has been in the country. . . . To the shop of his cousin or uncle come all sorts of people, men of all nations, south Germans, north Germans, Jews, Irish, Americans, English.[7]

For the newcomer, working in a relative's store was an introduction both to America and to the business world. The relative, who had arrived in

America earlier, helped the newcomer, while bene-
fiting from his labor at the same time. However, a
newcomer could not remain a mere clerk forever,
and a process evolved that enabled him to become
established:

> After two years the young peasant lad has be-
> come a proper clerk; that is, he speaks English
> well and understands the business from top
> to bottom. His pay has climbed from four to
> eight dollars a month, and it is now time to
> look for a better position. His relative actually
> helps him look about and he ends up in the
> place of another German where things operate
> on a larger scale. The [relative] does not lose
> thereby, for he simply imports another lad
> who starts at four dollars a month.
>
> After four [more] years it occurs to the
> clerk to set up in business for himself. He has
> saved up a hundred or two hundred dollars
> and found a friend who has as much again.
> One fine Sunday, the two are off to see the
> grocer with whom they served their apprentice-
> ships. The grocer notices what is up at once.
> The back room, behind the shop, is opened
> and a flask of good old brandy loosens
> tongues. The two have learned that the grocer
> has opened a new enterprise or that he con-
> templates investing in a wholesale house, and
> they have come to purchase his store. Natur-
> ally the few hundred dollars are not enough;

but the relative will give them credit for the rest, and with the last glass the bargain is sealed. . . . After a few years they have paid off their debts, and in a few more each partner owns his own store.[8]

Immigrant self-help organizations and relatives willing to sponsor new arrivals made the transition from northern Europe to America easier for many who came to the New World, though the adjustment was never *easy*. Wherever they came from—Scandinavia, Germany, Flanders, Holland, or France—the newcomers were strangers to America, confronting an alien culture and, in most cases, a language they didn't understand.

A Swedish farmer coming to a small farm community in Minnesota made up of fellow Swedes faced little difficulty in fitting in. But in the cities, where all sorts of immigrant groups lived side by side with established American families, the raw immigrant, obviously foreign, was often an object of scorn. Often the alienation felt by new immigrants was overwhelming, as one German-American observer noted:

The German in America is a complete stranger. Everything is strange, the country, the climate, laws and customs. One ought to realize what it means to be an alien in a far distant land. More than this, the German in America is despised as alien, and he must often hear the nickname "Dutchman," at least until he learns to speak English fluently. It is horrible what the German immigrant must endure from the Americans, Irish, and English. . . . Only in places where the Germans are in the majority does the newly arrived immigrant find, after all the hardships of the journey, an endurable existence.[9]

To become in the majority, immigrants tended to congregate in neighborhoods where people from the Old World could create a little of what they had left behind. Their neighbors spoke their language, the stores sold the kinds of goods they were used to, and traditional holidays could be observed with the same spirit and gusto. In Cincinnati in the nineteenth century, for example, almost fifty thousand Germans lived in a section of the city called "Over the Rhine." The same pattern was repeated in St. Louis, Milwaukee, almost everywhere immigrants tended to settle. One visitor to New York City in the 1860s described its German section, then called *Kleindeutschland*, or Little Germany:

New York has about 120,000 German-born inhabitants. Two-thirds of these live in Kleindeutschland. They come from every part of Germany. . . . Naturally the Germans were not forced by the authorities, or by law, to settle in this specific area. It just happened. . . . The Germans like to live together; this permits them to speak their own language and live according to their own customs.

Life in Kleindeutschland is almost the same as in the Old Country. Bakers, butchers, druggists—all are Germans. There is not a single business which is not run by Germans. Not only the shoe-makers, tailors, barbers, physicians, grocers, and innkeepers are German, but the pastors and priests as well. There is even a German lending library where one can get all kinds of German books. The residents of Kleindeutschland need not even know English in order to make a living. . . .[10]

Immigrants tended to feel comfortable in neighborhoods like these. Their children, however, often felt different. They found themselves torn between two worlds—an America that demanded conformity to get ahead and the desires of their immigrant parents to pass on their European heritage. The result was often confusion and shame, as one college-educated daughter of a German immigrant expressed:

My father made me learn German and always was wanting me to read it. I hated to have anything to do with it. It seemed to me something inferior. People in the West call a thing "Dutch" as a term of scorn. It was not till I was in college that I realized what German literature and philosophy have meant to the world, and that to be a German is not a thing to be ashamed of.[11]

Tensions like these, between generations, fostered the process of assimilation through which the children of immigrants could more easily enter the American mainstream. Old habits die hard, however, and the immigrant neighborhoods, sitting like ever-shrinking ethnic islands in an American sea, survived to give comfort and shelter to new arrivals.

Chapter 10

Reaction and Rebellion

Beginning in the 1830s some segments of American society began to see massive immigration as a threat. Many of the newcomers were Catholics, while most Americans at the time were Protestants. Immigrants also took jobs away from American workers. Still others feared the political ideas of some immigrants or disliked them because of prejudice.

In the three decades before the Civil War, anti-immigrant feeling broke out with a ferocity and violence America had never seen before, lasting until well into the twentieth century. In 1831, for example, an anti-Catholic mob burned down the Ursuline Convent in Charlestown, Massachusetts. A mob raged through the Catholic neighborhoods of Philadelphia in 1844. While few outbursts of anti-immigrant feeling reached this level, anti-

118

immigrant activity, in whatever form, came to be known by a single word: nativism.

Nativist outbursts became more common in the 1840s and '50s. In 1848 two events combined to attract even more immigration to America: the discovery of gold in California and a series of revolutions that swept through virtually every country in Europe. The political refugees who came, called Forty-Eighters, brought with them democratic ideals developed during their struggles against the aristocracies of Europe. Relatively few in number, they were college-educated intellectuals whose radical ideas—ranging from anarchy to communism (the *Communist Manifesto* was written in 1848) to constitutional democracy—tended to become identified with immigrants of the same nationalities. German Forty-Eighters became a particular target of attack. A nativist book published in 1856 called *Immigration: Its Evils and Consequences* includes this passage:

> To borrow the language of that bold and fearless champion of the American reformation (Hon. Wm. R. Smith [a prominent nativist leader]), "The mass of foreigners who come to this country are incapable of appreciating the policies of our government, they do not sufficiently understand our institutions. Patriotism is natural in a native, but it must be cultivated in a foreigner. Their minds are filled with a vague and indefinite idea of liberty. . . ."

[The Germans'] demands are antagonistic to the fundamental principles and established usages of government. . . . The presidency is to be abolished, all powers are to be vested exclusively in the masses, and the Constitution must give way to the whims and caprices of the people. . . . They [Germans] have boldly entered the political arena, asserted their right to share with us in legislation and with a zeal and determination worthy of a better cause, sought to engraft upon our institutions the "principles which they imbibed in early youth." The abjuration of the allegiance to the country of their birth has not divested them of their principles. The oath of allegiance to ours has not infused into them the spirit of our government.[1]

In addition many opponents of unrestricted immigration argued that cheap foreign labor drove down the wages of American workers. Nativist advocates saw European newcomers as an unfair supplement to the labor market—one that would eventually drive established Americans into poverty. In an 1856 anti-immigrant book, author Thomas Whitney expressed a point of view that would be repeated, in different forms, for generations to come:

Before the unequal competition of immigrant labor cast its shadow over the industrial interests of our country, every American journeyman mechanic was enabled, by the force of his industry, to maintain a financial position equal to that of his social, moral and political tradition. He was sure of employment, at wages adapted to the dignity of his franchise. . . . But with a superabundant immigration from Europe came a train of evils which are now rapidly developing themselves. . . . How vast the number of those who have been driven from their employments to make room for the under-bidding competition of foreign labor! The American mechanic cannot live upon the pittance demanded by his European competitor. It is not his custom—it was not the custom of his fathers—it is degrading to his sense of self-respect.[2]

Nativism became such a powerful political issue that the proponents of anti-immigration policies formed their own political party, the Native American party, in 1845. Pledging themselves to the "defence of American institutions against the encroachments of foreign influence, open or concealed,"[3] the Native Americans—or Know-Nothings as they came to be called because of a secret password they used—became a real political force. The Know-Nothings won control of six state governments, and their candidate for President in 1856, ex-President Millard Fillmore, collected nearly 22 percent of the votes cast. Yet the party's platform was based on little more than an open hatred of immigrants:

> The danger of foreign influence, threatening a gradual destruction of our national institutions, failed not to arrest the attention of the Father of his Country in the very dawn of American liberty. . . . It is an incontrovertible truth, that the civil institutions of the United States of America have been seriously affected, and that they now stand in imminent peril from the rapid and enormous increase of the body of residents of foreign birth, imbued with foreign feelings, and of an ignorant and immoral character. . . .[4]

Much of the attraction that the Know-Nothing platform held was due to a liberal naturalization law passed by Congress in 1825. The law allowed immigrants to become citizens—with full voting rights—after a much shorter residence than previous laws. As a result some immigrants—especially in the large cities—fell under the influence of political bosses who, in return for the immigrant's vote, helped him to adjust to the shock of immigration and got him past the obstacles of government bureaucracy. Not all immigrants came under the thumb of political bosses, however, and most Americans were repelled by the ideas of the Know-

Nothings. Asked in 1855 whether he was sympathetic to the Know-Nothings, Abraham Lincoln said:

> How could I be? How can any one who abhors the oppression of negroes, be in favor of degrading classes of white people? Our progress in degeneracy appears to me to be pretty rapid. As a nation, we began by declaring that "*all men are created equal.*" We now practically read it, "all men are created equal, *except negroes.*" When the Know-Nothings get control, it will read, "all men are created equal, except negroes, *and foreigners and catholics.*" When it comes to this I should prefer emigrating to some country where they make no pretence of loving liberty—to Russia, for instance, where despotism can be taken pure, and without the base alloy of hypocracy.[5]

Each immigrant group responded differently to nativists' attacks. The Irish, for example, organized themselves politically and, where their numbers were large enough, captured control of the political machines. For most German immigrants—the largest northern European ethnic group—the response to nativism was quite different. Most Germans, rather than striking back, retreated into their own communities, forming a kind of psychological "stockade" that offered security against the prejudices of the nativists. A small number of German-American immigrants did fight back against the rising tide of antiforeign feeling, however, and the most famous of those was a Forty-Eighter named Carl Schurz.

Schurz was born in the village of Liblar, near Cologne, in 1829. He studied at the University of Bonn, and went on to publish a liberal newspaper sympathetic to the democratic ideals sweeping through Germany and the rest of Europe. When revolution broke out in 1848, Schurz fought on the side of the democratic revolutionaries. He fled to Switzerland the following year, and in 1852 emigrated to the United States. After living in Philadelphia for a few years, Schurz moved to Wisconsin, where he became associated with the newly formed Republican party.

Schurz was a talented writer and orator, and he used these skills to support Republican candidates around the country, campaigning for Abraham Lincoln in both 1858 and 1860. In a famous speech called "True Americanism," which he delivered many times, Schurz not only demolished the ideas of the nativists, but he went on to show his audiences that to be antiforeign was to undermine the very principles on which America was founded. Declaring that "I, too, am an American citizen,"[6] Schurz began his oration by telling his listeners what America meant to him as a boy growing up in Germany:

I, born in a foreign land, pay my tribute to Americanism? Yes, for to me the word "Americanism," *true* "Americanism," comprehends the noblest ideas which ever swelled a human heart with noble pride.

It is one of the earliest recollections of my boyhood that one summer night our whole village was stirred up by an uncommon occurrence. . . . That night our neighbors were pressing around a few wagons covered with linen sheets and loaded with household utensils and boxes and trunks to their utmost capacity. One of our neighboring families was moving far away across a great water, and it was said they would never again return. And I saw silent tears trickling down weather-beaten cheeks, and the hands of rough peasants firmly pressing each other, and some of the men and women hardly able to speak when they nodded to one another a last farewell. At last the train started into motion, they gave three cheers for *America,* and then in the first gray dawn of the morning I saw them wending their way over the hill until they disappeared in the shadow of the forest. . . .

That was the first time that I heard of America, and my childish imagination took possession of a land covered partly with majestic trees, partly with flowery prairies, immeasurable to the eye, and intersected with large rivers and broad lakes—a land where everybody could do what he thought best, and where nobody need be poor because everybody was free.[7]

He went on to tell his audience how, in 1848, he participated in a revolution aimed at bringing democracy to his native land. When that effort failed, he set out for America, determined to help preserve democracy there. And immigrants like himself, he told his audience, were helping to do just that:

> Under this banner [American democracy] all the languages of civilized mankind are spoken, every creed is protected, every right is sacred. There stands every element of Western society, with enthusiasm for a great cause, with confidence in each other, with honor to themselves. This is the banner floating over the glorious valley which stretches from the western slope of the Alleghenies to the Rocky Mountains. . . . The inscription on that banner is . . . "Liberty and equal rights, common to all as the air of heaven—liberty and equal rights, one and inseparable! . . ."
>
> This is true Americanism, clasping mankind to its great heart. Under its banner we march; let the world follow.[8]

Through speeches like these Carl Schurz helped his fellow immigrants gain acceptance in American society. At the time Schurz traveled around the country for the Republican party, however, anti-foreignism and the Know-Nothings were already on the decline. In place of those issues, the question of slavery dominated national debates. Soon the Civil War would decide the question. And when the war did break out, President Lincoln rewarded Carl Schurz for his efforts on behalf of the anti-slavery Republicans, first by appointing Schurz U.S. minister to Spain, and then by giving him a commission as a brigadier general in the Union Army. Eventually Schurz was promoted to major general, commanding troops at such major Civil War battles as Bull Run, Chancellorsville, and Gettysburg.

Like Schurz, most northern European immigrants were opposed to slavery, although many of them accepted the view of the day that blacks were inferior to whites. Some immigrants were horrified by the slave system, which they considered to be a moral outrage, while others, though opposed to it, remained relatively indifferent. No matter how immigrants felt about slavery, however, they were enthusiastic in support of their new country. When fighting broke out, immigrants quickly and unhesitatingly gave their support to the section, North or South, in which they lived. Since most immigrants lived in the North, though, most of them supported the Union cause. Typical of the patriotic support that the Union received from northern European immigrants was this advertisement in a Swedish-language newspaper shortly after the outbreak of the war:

To the Scandinavians of Minnesota!

It is high time for us, as a people, to arise with sword in hand, and fight for our adopted country and for liberty.

This country is in danger. A gigantic power has arisen against it and at the same time against liberty and democracy, in order to crush them. . . . This land which we, as strangers, have made our home, has received us with friendship and hospitality. We enjoy equal privileges with the native-born. . . . The law protects and befriends us all alike. We have also sworn allegiance to the same.

Countrymen, "Arise to arms; our adopted country calls." Let us prove ourselves worthy of that land, and of those heroes from whom we descend.[9]

In a similarly patriotic tract, a German-language newspaper, the *Illinois Staats-Zeitung,* expressed the reasons behind the pro-Union fervor shared by many German immigrants:

The German hates the flag of the rebels, and this hate knows no bounds; he will never fight under the flag of secessionists; on the contrary, he will take up arms against it, even when confronted by superior forces.

The hatred of the German race toward everything that savors of slavery is deadly. No doubt it emanates from the fact that the Germans are primarily a working people, who are very practical in everything they undertake, and that they have implicit trust in the possibility that some day humanity may be entirely freed from despotism, whether it be political, religious, or economic.[10]

Every kind of immigrant was welcomed by the Union army—the North needed able men to fight the war. At first, immigrant soldiers were organized into distinctive ethnic units, often commanded by their countrymen. One German unit was so inspired by the promotion of its general, Franz Sigel, to high command that it coined the phrase "I fights mit Sigel"—later in the war, the slogan became a byword for the bravery of German-American soldiers.

What was life like for the recent immigrant who fought in the Civil War? It was much like that of any other soldier, except that service in the army brought recent immigrants into contact with other Americans. As they fought side by side, these encounters helped to break down the nativist feelings some Americans may have had. After all, the immigrants were fighting—and dying—for the same cause as they, and they showed great bravery in the field.

Jan Vogel's experience was typical of many northern European immigrants who fought in the Civil War. Vogel immigrated to Michigan from the Netherlands in the mid-1850s. In 1861, when President Lincoln issued a call for volunteers, Vogel, together with twenty-four other Dutchmen, enlisted in the Michigan cavalry. Vogel saw action throughout the war and was wounded several times, as he recalled in his memoirs:

> On October 7, 1864 I received a gunshot wound in my forehead, three inches above my right eye. I fell from my horse but was assigned to safety. My wound, cleansed and treated by a skillful regimental surgeon, healed so rapidly that in the following month I was able to report for duty. . . . On November 30, 1864, a general engagement began in which at about 3 p.m. a musket ball passed through my left leg four inches above the ankle. Together with my good Dutch friend Martin de Groot who was slightly wounded, I rode 14 miles on horseback that same evening. . . . The following morning we proceeded toward Nashville, four miles distant but experienced great difficulty riding because of our wounds. . . . The city of Nashville at this moment was surrounded by a rebel army while our forces stationed within were endeavoring to hold it.[11]

Vogel managed to get into Nashville where he was assigned to a hospital. Two weeks later he was transferred to another hospital in the North, but by this time his wound had developed gangrene. For a while it seemed that the leg might have to be amputated. The wound eventually healed, and Vogel was discharged as a sergeant on August 1, 1865, in the city of Detroit.

Vogel's experiences in the Civil War, like those of thousands of others, brought about a considerable change in the attitudes toward immigrants. They had responded to the call to save the Union, and had fought alongside native-born Americans. The anti-foreign prejudices that had swept the nation prior to the Civil War continued to exist, but they were more muted and less widespread. No longer could the nativists argue that the immigrants were a disloyal element who threatened America's democratic institutions.

Chapter 11

Immigration in the Gilded Age

In the years following the Civil War, the United States changed dramatically. At the outbreak of the war, the country had been mostly agricultural, although the North was already well on the way toward industrialization. By the early years of the twentieth century, however, America had been transformed from a mainly agricultural society to the world's leading industrial nation. Unskilled labor, entrepreneurial energy, and technological talent were necessary to bring about this change. Immigrants from northern Europe and their children helped to provide all three.

Northern European immigrants became more accepted in American society in the last decades of the nineteenth century. This change in American attitudes came about not so much because nativists had a change of heart, but because they feared another kind of immigrant. Between 1820 and 1930 over 37.5 million immigrants came to America in ever-increasing waves: Between 1820 and 1860, 5 million came; between 1860 and 1890, 13.5 million arrived; and between 1890 and 1930, the total was almost 19 million. The first two waves came primarily from the British Isles and the northern European countries. The last wave was made up mostly of people from southern and eastern European countries—Italians, Slavs, Russian Jews, and others. This latter wave seemed so foreign, not only to native-born Americans but also to northern Europeans, that much of the hatred that was formerly reserved for northern European immigrants was aimed at these groups.

By the 1870s the northern Europeans of the first wave of immigration had become integrated into American society. Some became captains of industry in an era when industrialists, unfettered by any sort of controls, wielded enormous power: Henry C. Frick became a force in steel manufacturing, and Frederick Weyerhaeuser carved out a lumber and timber empire; George Westinghouse and Charles P. Steinmetz were instrumental in the development of the electrical industry; H. J. Heinz and Carl A. Swanson became bywords in prepared foods; Bausch and Lomb in optics; Charles Pfizer in pharmaceuticals; and Claus Spreckels in sugar refining.

Most northern Europeans in the United States, however, were working people, and they paid a heavy price for America's industrial growth. Prior to the Civil War, most working people had special talents that made it possible for them to bargain with their employers for adequate wages and working conditions. A craftsman who was unhappy with his or her employer could leave that job behind knowing that it was an easy matter to find another. Skilled workers were always in demand.

All of this changed with the coming of machine production. A skilled worker was no longer needed to manufacture a product. Instead, almost anybody could be taught to operate a machine within a few days. And if a worker did not like the wages and working conditions, his employer did not much care if he left. Someone else was always willing to take his place.

As a result, America in the last decades of the nineteenth century was periodically convulsed by labor unrest and violent strikes. The first of these was a series of incidents in 1877 that ended in a nationwide railroad strike. Since the railroads were the main arteries of industry, production nearly came to a halt and troops were called out to restore order. Afterward *The North American Review* published an article by "a striker" in which a Scandinavian worker said:

> Forty years ago my father came over to this country from Sweden. He had a small business and a large family. In Europe business does not grow as fast as children come, and poverty over there is an inheritance. He heard that North

America was peopled and governed by working men, and the care of the states was mainly engaged in the welfare and prosperity of labor. That moved him, and so I came to be born here. He, and millions like him, made this country their home, and their homes have mainly made this country what it is. . . .

So it was before the war, but since then, it seems to me, the power has got fixed so long in one set of hands [the industrialists'] that things are settling down into a condition like what my father left behind him in Europe forty years ago, and what stands there still. I mean the slavery of labor.[1]

The striker then set out a brief list of what working people wanted. Today these demands seem only what a working person might reasonably expect in exchange for his labor. But in the nineteenth century, such lists struck fear among the industrial barons of the Gilded Age.

Our claim is simple. We demand *fair wages*.

We say that the man able and willing to work, and for whom there is work to do, is entitled to wages sufficient to provide him with enough food, shelter, and clothing to sustain and preserve his health and strength. We contend that the employer has no right to speculate on starvation when he reduces wages below a living figure, saying, if we refuse that remuneration, there are plenty of starving men out of work that will gladly accept half a loaf instead of no bread.

We contend that to regard the laboring class in this manner is to consider them as the captain of a slave-ship regards his cargo, who throws overboard those unable to stand their sufferings. Let those who knew the South before the war go now amongst the mining districts of Pennsylvania, and compare the home of the white laborer with the quarters of the slave; let them compare the fruits of freedom with the produce of slavery.[2]

Working people began to organize labor unions. The best-known were the Knights of Labor and the American Federation of Labor—but opposition to trade unionism was intense. Businessmen, who were committed to the unregulated economic system of the time, vehemently denounced unions. They claimed that unions would disrupt the economic system and threaten the rights of property owners. Farmers, professionals, the press, and the clergy agreed.

Nonetheless, working people continued to organize trade unions. It was clear that something had to be done to improve conditions. Until World War I, for example, the typical workweek lasted six days, and in some industries seven. The workday ranged from ten to fourteen hours despite efforts to reduce it to eight. Wages were low, and in times of economic recession, employers did not hesitate to cut wages even further. Since businesses were free to run their affairs without regulation, industrial accidents were common. A study estimated that in 1913, there were 25,000 workers killed and approximately 700,000 hurt or disabled on the job.

Most American workers who joined unions or went out on strike were not challenging the American system itself—they merely wanted to share in the profits of industry by receiving a living wage. A small minority of workers, however, wanted to dismantle the capitalist system completely, and replace it with a socialist or communist structure. Since Karl Marx, the founder of communism, was German, it is not surprising that many of these labor radicals were German-Americans who had become adherents of Marx's doctrines while still in Germany. Another radical doctrine that attracted some German-Americans was anarchy. Where the Marxists believed that capitalism should be replaced by a socialist form of government, the anarchists believed that all government was repressive and should be destroyed.

From the 1860s through the 1880s, Chicago was the center of left-wing labor activity. German, Austrian, and French radicals attempted to develop a revolutionary spirit among the workers of Chicago, at least half of whom were immigrants. They had little influence, actually, but their fiery words, which emphasized force, frightened many Americans. The platform of the International Working People's Association was often a call to revolt:

> This system capitalism is unjust, insane, and murderous. Therefore those who suffer under it, and do not wish to be responsible for its continuance, ought to strive for its destruction by all means and with their utmost energy. . . . It is therefore self-evident that the fight of proletarianism against the bourgeoisie must have a violent revolutionary character. . . . There is only one remedy left—force. . . . Agitation to organize, organizations for the purpose of rebellion, this is the course if the workingmen would rid themselves of their chains.[3]

Radicals like these attracted only small followings and, if ignored, probably would have had very little effect on immigrant working people. However, an incident occurred in 1886 which left the impression in the public's mind that every German-American was a bomb-throwing anarchist out to destroy American society. That incident was the Haymarket Square bombing in Chicago.

The Haymarket Square affair had its roots in the movement among labor groups to win the right to an eight-hour workday. In the early part of 1886, thousands of workers were on strike over this issue around the country. In late April workers at the McCormick Harvester Works in Chicago went on strike for an eight-hour day. At a strike demonstration in front of the factory a few days later, police opened fire on the strikers, killing four of them and wounding many more. August Spies, a German anarchist who was addressing the crowd when the shooting occurred, was quick to call a protest meeting in Haymarket Square. In a circular Spies hastily drew up, he wrote:

> WORKINGMEN, TO ARMS!!!
>
> The masters sent out their bloodhounds—the police; they killed six of your brothers at McCormicks this afternoon. They killed the poor wretches because they, like you, had the courage to disobey the supreme will of your bosses. They killed them because they dared ask for the shortening of the hours of toil. They killed them to show you, "Free American Citizens" that you must be satisfied and contented with whatever your bosses condescend to allow you, or you will get killed.[4]

Many workers came to the meeting at Haymarket Square, and the police came too—hundreds of them. When the police attempted to break up the meeting, someone—no one knows who—threw a bomb into the middle of the police ranks, killing seven policemen and wounding sixty more. Many Americans were convinced that the bomb was the work of the German anarchists. Six of the eight men arrested for the Haymarket bombing—on very flimsy evidence— had German surnames. To some, that alone was proof that they had been behind the bombing. A popular cartoon figure of the era portrayed a long-haired, wild-eyed German anarchist bomb-thrower, and this caricature came to be a symbol for all German immigrants. Of the men arrested for the Haymarket bombing, four were executed, but three others were pardoned by the Governor of Illinois, John Peter Altgeld, who was an immigrant himself.

The Haymarket affair resulted in a backlash against German immigrants. The American Protective Association was founded in 1887 in Iowa, dedicated to "protecting" Americans from the foreign-born. In 1894 five wealthy Bostonians founded the Immigration Restriction League, aimed at enacting legislation that would shut America's doors to foreign immigration. Headed by Senator Henry Cabot Lodge, the league became influential, and eventually it succeeded in enacting the quota system for immigrants that it sought, although it took twenty-five years.

Typical of the antiforeign feeling that the Haymarket affair generated was this article in the influential *North American Review*:

> Mr. Seward [U.S. senator from New York] once declared that of all the elements which entered into our national composition the German was the element which he most feared. The discontented and revolutionary spirit which characterizes the German mind, coupled

with the little learning which every citizen of the Fatherland brings with him, and the clannishness of his race, seemed to Mr. Seward a danger menacing to the existing order of things. It is indeed true that the German combines in his nature traits dangerous to the fundamental principles of the present system of our society. . . .

Mr. Seward's fears apply pertinently to a large part of the 6,000,000 Germans who now form a portion of the American Union. Of these the Socialists justly claim large numbers, and, if we examine the first acts and constitution of the Socialistic Labor Party, it will appear that from its very foundation the chief officials and ringleaders of the organization were and still are Germans, not a few of whom have been expelled or have fled from their native country because of conspiracy against society. Nevertheless, these men have become the leaders of a great national and American movement. . . .[5]

Nativist outbursts like this were not successful in stopping the labor movement. In 1886 two cigar makers, Samuel Gompers and Adolph Strasser—the latter of German origin—founded the American Federation of Labor. Unlike the anarchists, the AFL concentrated on "bread-and-butter issues" like wages, hours, and working conditions. It was an effective labor organization, one that found—for the first time—a permanent niche for organized labor in the nation.

Other labor organizations remained active as well. In 1894 workers at the Pullman factory in Chicago went on strike over a series of wage cuts, some of them as much as fifty percent. Most of the workers lived in company-owned houses. When the wage cut went into effect, the Pullman Company, which made railroad cars, refused to reduce rents proportionately—and the workers walked out. Some of the Pullman workers belonged to the American Railway Union, which claimed 150,000 members, and they appealed to it for support. Eugene V. Debs, head of the union, told his members not to handle trains that carried Pullman cars. As a result, national railroad traffic was disrupted, and troops were called into Chicago by President Grover Cleveland to end the strike and get the trains moving again.

Despite setbacks, trade unionism continued to grow, and northern European immigrants supplied much of its membership and leadership. But northern Europeans no longer made up the bulk of newcomers seeking to find a new life in America. In 1882, for example, 788,000 immigrants entered the United States, 350,000 of whom came from Great Britain and northern Europe. That year, only 32,000 immigrants came from Italy and 17,000 from Russia. By 1907, when 1,285,000 immigrants entered the country, only 116,000 of them were from the British Isles and northern Europe; 258,000

Russians entered the country in 1907, along with 285,000 Italians.

But the decline in the volume of northern European immigration did not mean that its presence was no longer felt. Every immigrant who entered New York Harbor after 1886 was greeted by the Statue of Liberty, a gift to the American people from the French. On it was inscribed the words of a poet of German-Jewish descent, Emma Lazarus:

> Give me your tired, your poor
> Your huddled masses yearning to breathe free,
> The wretched refuse of your teeming shore,
> Send these, the homeless, tempest-tost to me,
> I lift my lamp beside the golden door!

Chapter 12

The Huddled Masses

By the late nineteenth century, America was flooded with immigrants arriving daily at Ellis Island. The federal government's reception station for immigrants was erected on an island in New York Harbor in 1890. And three northern European immigrants played a crucial role in making America more receptive to all immigrants: Carl Schurz, Thomas Nast, and Jacob Riis.

As mentioned previously, Schurz was a German Forty-Eighter who arrived in America in 1852 and quickly rose to prominence as a confidant of Abraham Lincoln, U.S. minister to Spain, and a major general in the Civil War. But Schurz's greatest contributions to American public life came after the Civil War. Between 1865 and 1868 Schurz was a journalist, for a time publishing the St. Louis *Westliche Post,* a German-language newspaper. In 1868 Schurz was elected to the U.S. Senate from

Missouri, serving with distinction for six years as the voice of liberal Republicanism. In 1877 President Rutherford B. Hayes appointed Schurz secretary of the interior.

Schurz had considerable influence throughout the late nineteenth century. At a time when national, state, and local politics were more corrupt than at any other point in American history, Schurz was an independent, honest politician whose idealism and crusading zeal for honest government provided an inspiring example to millions of Americans, newcomers and native-born alike. Schurz supported civil service reform, for example, which sought to end the federal patronage system and replace it with a system in which government employees were hired on merit alone. Schurz was so influential that one historian called him "the self-constituted but exceedingly useful incarnation of our national conscience."[1]

Besides his political posts, Schurz was the editor in chief of the *New York Evening Post* from 1881 to 1884 and editorial writer for *Harper's Weekly* from 1892 to 1898. Many of Schurz's writing and speeches defended the recently arrived immigrant. As an immigrant who had become one of the best-known Americans of his day, Schurz explained to native-born Americans that immigrants, far from being a threat to the nation, were, in fact, helping to build the country.

Typical of Schurz's writing about immigrants was an 1869 piece defending foreign-language newspapers against nativist criticism that charged they

were proof of the immigrants' unwillingness to adapt
to American ways:

> It may well be in place here to say a word
> about a prejudice entertained by some well-
> meaning Americans, that the publication of
> newspapers . . . in any language other than
> English, is an undesirable, if not positively
> dangerous, practice. It is said that it prevents
> immigrants from learning the language of the
> country; that it fosters the cultivation of un-
> American principles, notions and habits, and
> that it thus stands in the way of a sound
> American patriotism in those coming from
> foreign lands to make their homes among
> us. . . . I have as much personal experience of
> the German-born population of the United
> States, its character, its aspirations, and its
> American patriotism as any person now living;
> and this experience enables me to affirm that
> the prejudice against the German-American
> press is groundless.[2]

Schurz went on to describe how many immigrants,
especially the elderly who found it difficult to learn
English, depended on foreign-language newspapers
to keep informed on the issues that concerned them
as American citizens. And should anyone doubt the
patriotism of the immigrant, Schurz wrote:

> I have already mentioned that there are many
> foreign-born citizens among us whose Ameri-

can patriotism is in one respect finer than that of many a native. This republic being the land of their choice, they want to be and to remain proud of that choice, and to have that pride recognized as just. A man of that class is as sensitive of any reason for casting a slur upon the character of the Republic, as a bridegroom would feel and resent a shadow cast upon the fair fame of his bride. More than once I have heard one of my countrymen, when anything discreditable to the American nation had happened, exclaim with a pathetic accent of sincerest grief: "Ah, what will they think of this in the old country! I hope they will never hear of it." And such true patriotic sighs were uttered, and perhaps felt, not in English, but in German.[3]

Like Schurz, Thomas Nast made his contribution to American public affairs with his pen—only Nast's talent was as a cartoonist, not as a writer. Nast was born in the town of Landau, Bavaria, in 1840. His father, a sergeant in the Bavarian army, was forced to flee with his family to America in 1846 because of his democratic views. From his early youth Nast displayed great drawing talent. At the age of fifteen he went to work as a draftsman for America's leading illustrated weekly newspaper, *Frank Leslie's Illustrated Weekly,* and six years later was hired as a staff artist at the newspaper for which he would do his greatest work—*Harper's Weekly,* which, in the

nineteenth century, had relatively the same circulation and appeal as *Time* and *Newsweek* do today.

Until the 1890s newspapers did not have the
technology to reproduce photographs. Instead, they
relied on their illustrators to provide readers with
graphic pictures of current events. Nast's drawings
of the Civil War for *Harper's Weekly* made him a
national celebrity, and his cartoons often seemed to
crystallize the political issues of the day. In fact,
Nast is considered to be the father of the American
political cartoon—he created the elephant and the
donkey as symbols for the Republican and Democratic parties.

But Nast's greatest achievement as a political
cartoonist came in the early 1870s. New York City
was controlled by a corrupt political machine headed
by William Marcy "Boss" Tweed. Like most urban
machines of the day, Tweed's empire was built on
the votes of the poor—mainly immigrants. Tweed's
machine organized the poor neighborhoods of the
city skillfully. In exchange for small favors, Tweed's
candidates got votes—enough to win control of the
New York City government. In less than eighteen
months, Boss Tweed and his friends looted the city
treasury of more than $30 million.

Nast was an advocate of honest government, and
he set out in his cartoons to undo what he called the
"Tweed Ring." In his cartoons in *Harper's Weekly,*
Nast alternately drew Tweed as a tiger devouring
the city, as a fat, bloated thief calmly looking on as
the city was plundered, and in his most famous

Tweed cartoon, as a vulture looking out over the city with his cronies, saying, "Let Us Prey." Where political reformers could not affect Tweed, Nast did. At one point in Nast's assault, Tweed is reported to have commented:

> Let's stop them damned pictures. I don't care so much what the papers write about me—my constituents can't read; but, damn it, they can see pictures![4]

Tweed offered Nast half a million dollars to leave the country; Nast refused. Ultimately, evidence was found of Tweed's corruption, and the ring was broken, largely due to Nast's cartoons. In an editorial, *The Nation* confirmed Tweed's fear of Nast's power:

> Mr. Nast has carried political illustrations during the last six months to a pitch of excellence never before attained in this country. . . . It is right to say that he brought the rascalities of the Ring home to hundreds of thousands who never would have looked at the figures and printed denunciations. . . .[5]

Nast became permanently identified with the late-nineteenth-century movement to reform municipal governments around the country. But his best-remembered legacy may be his creation for *Harper's Weekly* of the figure of a jolly old man with a pipe and a beard, a figure based on the folklore of his native Germany. It was Nast who first drew Santa Claus in the form we know him today.

Like Schurz and Nast, Jacob Riis made a name for himself as a journalist. Born in Ribe, Denmark, in 1849, Riis left home at the age of twenty-one after he realized that the social-caste system in Denmark prevented him from marrying the woman he loved. Riis was from a poor family, and the girl he loved—whom he did eventually marry—was the daughter of one of the richest men in town.

Riis, who had been trained as a carpenter, thought that making his fortune in the New World would be an easy matter. Within a few weeks after he arrived in America, all his money was gone, and he was unable to find steady work. For the next three years Riis drifted from job to job, seldom working at one long enough to earn enough money to live on and often going hungry. Years later he recalled how despondent an immigrant's life could be:

> There was until last winter a doorway in Chatham Square [in New York] . . . which I could never pass without recalling those nights of hopeless misery with the policeman's periodic "Get up there! move on!" reenforced by a prod of his club or the toe of his boot. I slept there, or tried to when crowded out of the tenements by their nastiness. . . . I was now too shabby to get work, even if there had been any to get. . . . I was finally and utterly alone in the city, with

the winter approaching and every shivering night in the streets reminding me that a time was rapidly coming when such a life as I led could no longer be endured.[6]

At last Riis found a decent job, and he made enough money to put himself through telegrapher's school, where he learned how to be a wire-service reporter. From there, Riis got a job as a reporter for the *New York Tribune,* eventually becoming the paper's police reporter, stationed across the street from the police headquarters on the Lower East Side, the city's tenement district.

Riis never forgot what it was like to be poor and alone in a strange country. Throughout his career as a journalist, he aroused public opinion against the abuses of the unsanitary, overcrowded tenement slums that were home to the majority of immigrants flooding into America.

Riis focused his attention on "Mulberry Bend," the most notorious slum in the city. While researching a story on violations of New York's overcrowding law, Riis was struck by the misery he saw.

We used to go in the small hours of the morning into the worst tenements to count noses and see if the law against overcrowding was violated, and the sights I saw there gripped my heart until I felt that I must tell of them, or burst, or turn anarchist, or something. "A man may be a man even in a palace" in modern New York

as in ancient Rome, but not in a slum tenement.
So it seemed to me, and in anger I looked
around for something to strike off his fetters
with.[7]

Riis wanted to take photographs of slum conditions so that everyone could see just how bad they
were. Unfortunately, there was so little light in the
poorly ventilated, dark buildings that the cameras
of the day wouldn't function. Then the flash camera
was invented, and Riis was enthusiastic. With the
new process he could go into the tenements and
bring back evidence of the evils they bred. Before
long, Riis was stalking the poor immigrant neighborhoods with his camera:

> What with one thing and another, and in spite
> of all obstacles, I got my pictures, and put
> some of them to practical use at once. I recall
> a midnight expedition to the Mulberry Bend
> with the sanitary police that had turned up a
> couple of characteristic cases of overcrowding.
> In one instance two rooms that should at most
> have held four or five sleepers were found to
> contain fifteen, a week-old baby among them.
> Most of them were lodgers and slept there for
> "five cents a spot." There was no pretense of
> beds. When the report was submitted to the
> Health Board the next day, it did not make
> much of an impression—these things rarely do,
> put in mere words—until my negatives, still

dripping from the dark-room, came to reen-
force them. From them there was no appeal. . . .
Neither the landlord's protests nor the tenant's
plea "went" in the face of the camera's evidence, and I was satisfied.[8]

In 1890 Riis published a book about the tenement
slums, titled *How the Other Half Lives*. For most
Americans the book, filled with Riis's evocative
photographs, provided their first real look at the
conditions poor people and immigrants had to
grapple with in American cities. *How the Other Half
Lives* became a best seller, and the conditions it
exposed helped to begin a movement to clean up the
slums.

Riis traveled around the country giving talks on
conditions in the tenements and showing slides of his
photographs. He helped to foster the new "settlement
house" movement which sought to set up houses in
America's poor neighborhoods where the poor could
come to get help. In New York City, Riis was instrumental in the small parks movement. In order to
eliminate overcrowding in the slums, Riis and his
fellow reformers wanted to build open parks, and in
one of his most satisfying accomplishments, New
York City, at Riis's urging, foreclosed all Mulberry
Bend—which was three acres in size—and turned it
into a park.

Riis also crusaded against child labor. New York
State law forbade any children under the age of

fourteen to work. The law was designed to allow
children to get an adequate education, but it was
ignored. Instead, the sweatshops of New York's
Lower East Side—overcrowded factories that
usually manufactured clothing—became all the
schooling that many immigrant children ever received. Riis wrote:

> I had been struggling with the problem of
> child-labor in some East Side factories, and was
> not making any headway. The children had
> certificates, one and all, declaring them to be
> "fourteen," and therefore fit to be employed. It
> was perfectly evident that they were not ten in
> scores of cases, but the employer shrugged his
> shoulders and pointed to the certificates. . . .
> There was no birth registry to fall back on
> [because the children were from immigrant
> families]; that end of it was neglected. There
> seemed to be no way of proving the fact, yet
> the fact was there and must be proven. My own
> children were teething at the time, and it gave
> me an idea. I got Dr. Tracy to write out . . .
> for me at what age the dog-teeth should appear,
> when the molars, etc. Armed with that I went
> into the factories and pried open the little
> workers' mouths. . . . Even allowing for the
> backwardness of the slum, it was clear that a
> child that had not yet grown its dog-teeth was
> not "fourteen," for they should have been cut
> at twelve at the latest.[9]

Through exposés like this, Riis came to have considerable influence among reform groups. His work on behalf of penniless immigrants—which grew out of his own experience as a young man arriving in America from Denmark—helped to ease the social problems that poor people faced in America's slums. The example of Riis, like Carl Schurz and Thomas Nast, showed how new Americans from northern Europe could make positive contributions to their adopted country.

Chapter 13

One Hundred Percent Americanism

Ever since the civil rights upheavals that the United States experienced in the 1960s, our society has accepted, and even applauded, the idea of cultural diversity and ethnic pride. Before that time, however, immigrants were expected to conform to an "American" standard. Newcomers—and especially their children—were under enormous pressure to stop speaking their native languages and to abandon their European customs.

In the nineteenth century these pressures were exerted informally. So many immigrants were pouring into America daily that the flood was impossible to control. American society needed these immigrants in the factories and on the farms, and if the immigrants seemed alien, the effects of learning English and adapting to the new country would be felt soon enough. With so many foreign-born in America, no one knew exactly what Americanism

156

was supposed to mean, aside from the idea that the newcomer owed his or her loyalty to the adopted country.

By the beginning of the twentieth century, however, America had become a different nation. The United States had grown from a small nation of farmers to the world's leading industrial power. The frontier, which had once attracted immigrants to till its soil, no longer existed—all of America's territory was occupied. America had become a world power. The great age of American expansionism was ended, and in its place, the country looked inward to discover what it meant to be an American.

As a result even more pressure was exerted on new immigrants to become "Americanized." Newcomers were expected to become good citizens, and increasingly that term meant that they should abandon all that they had brought with them and adapt to the American Anglo-Saxon norm. That pressure was often reinforced by the inevitable clash of cultures that arose when one immigrant group came in contact with another. Hjordis Mortenson moved to Brooklyn with her family from Norway in the early part of the twentieth century. Looking back on her adjustment to America, she reflected:

> When we came here we had it a little hard in the beginning. We came to a very depressed area, not what we were used to from Norway at all, and we lived in a most undesirable neighborhood, which made it rather difficult.

So it was quite a change when we came to this country where there were so many people of so many other nationalities, speaking different tongues and different ways and different cultures. . . .

I started public school down in the Red Hook section of Brooklyn. It was a little difficult at the beginning because it was mostly Italians and Irish settlers there. I was the only Norwegian in the class. Being the only foreigner practically in the class, Scandinavian I mean, there was a little harassment. I was called a dumb squarehead and things like that. We did not speak English when we came here and that made it probably more difficult because there was nobody else in the class that could speak my language.[1]

At the same time, nativist groups continued to introduce legislation into Congress to limit European immigration. Most Americans resisted nativist pressure through the first decade and a half of the twentieth century—a period in American history called the Progressive Era—but in 1914 the beginning of World War I ultimately gave the nativists the upper hand.

When the war broke out, most Americans assumed that it was just another European war and none of their concern. The government, under the leadership of President Woodrow Wilson, officially proclaimed America's neutrality and reaffirmed the belief that the United States would not become involved. But it was difficult for Americans to remain aloof, especially for those who had ties to Europe. Virtually all white Americans could point to a European connection in their past. Ethnic attachments came to the surface strongly, even among Americans whose families had been in America since colonial times. Try as they might, Americans could not remain neutral for long.

As the war progressed in Europe, Anglo-Americans and those with some tie to the other Allied powers, France and Russia, came out in their support. German-Americans and those with ties to the other Central Powers, chiefly the Austro-Hungarian Empire, were equally fervent in their support of that side in the war. However, most Americans supported the Allies, especially after stories circulated of German atrocities in Belgium, which the German armies had conquered.

As American sympathies shifted toward the Allies, German-Americans, most of whom made no secret of their support of Germany, became more and more suspect. Many people came to see them as potential traitors and spies who, while they lived in the United States, owed their loyalty to the fatherland. For their part, most German-Americans could not bring themselves to believe that the stories of German atrocities and barbarism in Belgium were true. They were proud of German culture and German traditions, and unaware, by and large, of the ruthless militarism of the regime in Germany.

Hermann Hagedorn, a German-American, left an account of what it was like for him to discover that the German culture which he loved so much—the music of Beethoven, the poetry of Goethe—could sink to the depths it did in the villages of Belgium:

> Nothing in the easygoing world in which I had come to maturity had prepared me to believe in the possibility . . . of such violence and destruction, such callous inhumanity, as every day summoned me to face anew. All I had read or heard about war had dealt with armies clashing on battlefields, with civilians generally at a safe distance and protected under international codes of war. . . . But here in Belgium was "hell"—they called it "frightfulness"—proclaimed as military policy; cities destroyed, regardless of civilian population; cathedrals, precious libraries, whole villages wantonly given to the torch, and, picked at random, hundreds of burghers [townspeople] shot in reprisal for some sniper's bullet. . . . The stories were no product of overheated minds, no "scurrilous lies" as my family insisted, and, I know, believed. Germany herself, through her commanding officers, proclaimed them, plastered them on the walls of public buildings, to warn and to deter.[2]

On April 2, 1917, the United States entered World War I on the side of the Allies. President Wilson's declaration of war placed most German-

Americans in an awkward position. Most of them had taken a firm pro-German position on the war, arguing, for example, that the United States was being lured into the war to help rescue British financial interests. Once the United States entered the war, however, the majority of German-Americans rallied to the colors. They joined the armed forces, bought war bonds, and helped the war effort in a variety of other ways.

Despite this, many non-Germans in the United States saw German-Americans as potential traitors and spies. As a result German-Americans and German culture in the United States paid a terrible price. The war set in motion a hysterical drive to wipe out everything German from American civilization. Suddenly anything German was considered evil, and German-Americans who had lived in peace with their neighbors were abused because of their origins. Anti-German hysteria reached absurd extremes. For example, some people advocated eliminating the Fahrenheit thermometer because of its German name; waiters in an Ohio town refused to serve German fried potatoes; the frankfurter was renamed the hot dog, and sauerkraut was dubbed "liberty cabbage."

But the anti-German reaction was not limited only to words: Often it became violent and ugly. "Patriotic" vigilantes began smashing the windows of stores with German names, and if a German-American was suspected of disloyalty, these groups brought the offender before a kangaroo court (a

mock court where usual legal proceedings are dis-
regarded) that would mete out harsh punishment.
Police and other authorities usually looked the other
way. Even casual criticism about the government
made in private could be dangerous. Ernest Meyer,
a University of Wisconsin student at the time, left
an account of how anti-German hysteria destroyed
the career of one of his professors:

> A professor of German, an alien, in the privacy
> of his own office, made a joke about the Liberty
> Loan button. He was speaking to a colleague;
> there was no one else in the room. The col-
> league, his pretended friend, carried the jest in
> outrage to the university authorities. . . . The
> professor was expelled, with wide publicity. The
> papers branded him as a spy. . . .
>
> The professor of German, blacklisted, could
> find employment nowhere. He had a wife and
> two children. He planted cabbages and toma-
> toes in corner lots and peddled them door to
> door. He hired himself out for odd jobs to the
> few who knew him and loved him. Often I saw
> him walking down the street with a great tank
> strapped to his shoulders. He was spraying
> trees. . . . His wife, an American girl, baked
> bread and sold it to the neighbors. . . . For two
> long, gray years.[3]

The United States government set up a propaganda machine during the war called the Committee
for Public Information. Headed by George Creel,

the committee promoted what it called "one hundred percent Americanism." For German-Americans, that phrase meant the eradication of their heritage and tradition.

World War I ended on November 11, 1918, barely eighteen months after America entered the fight. But in that short period of time, the anti-German hysteria left deep scars. German-Americans had fought hard during the war to prove their loyalty. Heroes like American flying ace Captain Eddie Rickenbacker and the head of the American forces in Europe, General John J. Pershing (the family name had been Pfoerschin), helped to demonstrate the patriotism of German-Americans. But a deep psychological wound had been inflicted on German-Americans. Their language, their culture, and their loyalty had been vehemently and cruelly attacked, and the long-range effect of these attacks was considerable. In his book, *Autobiography of a Hyphenated American,* Walter V. Woehlke described how anti-Germanism during World War I affected him:

> Three years ago I believed that I was full-fledged American, as indistinguishably merged in the stream of American life as one drop of clear water merges with the other. I should have known better. The experiences of my early years should have taught me that the immigrant can no more turn himself into a 100 percent American than the rabbit can grow a

mane. . . . The immigrant must always remain a citizen of the second class.

. . . Loyal as I am, devoted as I am in the main, I am no longer as wholeheartedly American as I was. . . . The melting pot may be a beneficent institution for those who leap into it—though I have my doubts even on that point—but it must inevitably be a source of weakness to the nation that tries to act as the solvent. Its work can never be perfectly done, the process of assimilation is never fully complete, and in times of deep crises, when national unity and homogeneity are of paramount importance, the danger of reversion to original types, of sharp fissures between antagonistic racial groups, becomes greatest.[4]

The anti-German hysteria that the war generated left the German-American community with a cautious attitude, and a conviction that it would not be caught in such a position again. They became reluctant to express themselves on controversial issues, and tended to support the isolationist attitude of most American leaders during the 1920s and 1930s. Perhaps the principles of the Steuben Society, a German-American patriotic group founded in 1919, best expressed the timidity of German-Americans following World War I. The Society sought to "foster a patriotic American spirit among all citizens," to encourage Germans to engage in "a better participation in public affairs," to "maintain the traditions of the nation, to keep alive the memory of the achievements of the pioneers of this country, and to enlighten the public on the important part played by the Germanic element in the making of America," and to "guide our citizens through the intricacies of public policies, to warn them against political intrigues, and to oppose alien-influenced government."

Another effect of World War I, although indirect, was the success of various nativist groups in establishing a quota system for immigration that drastically reduced the number of foreign-born people allowed to enter the United States. This legislation came not so much from the war itself, but from an event that occurred in the final year of the conflict: the Russian Revolution. The success of the Bolsheviks in Russia in 1917 frightened many people in the United States. The Russian Communists advocated a worldwide revolution, and many wondered if the flood of eastern European immigration that resumed after the war carried the seeds of a Bolshevik upheaval in America.

One of those who got carried away by fear of the "Red Menace" was Attorney General A. Mitchell Palmer, who authorized federal agents to begin a wholesale roundup of suspected radicals in 1919 and 1920. These "Palmer raids" resulted in the arrest of more than six thousand people, almost all of them foreign-born. Those who could prove that they had become United States citizens were held for trial; those who could not were deported to the country they had emigrated from.

The Russian Revolution and the Palmer raids gave the nativists all the ammunition they needed to restrict immigration. In 1921 President Warren G. Harding signed a bill into law that set up a quota system for immigration. Under the quota, immigration was limited to three percent of the foreign-born population from a given country as of the 1910 census. Under the terms of this law, only 350,000 immigrants could legally enter the United States each year.

The quota law was designed to preserve the ethnic composition of America as it was then. Since most Americans were descended from people from northwestern Europe—the British Isles, France, Germany, Scandinavia, and Holland—the drafters of the legislation hoped to preserve that blend by enacting a law that would favor immigrants from those countries. After a close examination of the 1910 census, however, they realized that that year was a high point for the kind of immigration they hoped to stop. As a result a new immigration bill was introduced in 1924 that used the 1890 census as its base and further limited immigration from three percent to two percent of the foreign-born population at that time.

The bill was passed in 1924 and became known as the Johnson-Reed Act. It was a triumph for nativism. Not only was the 1910 census replaced by the 1890 census as the basis on which to establish a quota, but rather than basing the percentage quota on foreign-born Americans, it was based on the "national origins" of Americans—a change that vastly favored British and northern European immigration. In a real sense the bill demonstrated the degree to which northern Europeans had become an integral part of the American population. They were the favored groups now, proclaimed in the debate over the bill as the "Nordic" base on which America was built.

But at the same time, the passage of the Johnson-Reed Act signaled a fundamental change in the American nation. Under the new law, a total of only 150,000 European immigrants were allowed to enter the United States legally each year. And even if the countries of northern Europe were favored under that arrangement, the law nevertheless ended the place America had held for hundreds of years as the refuge for the world's poor and oppressed.

Chapter 14

Between the Wars

The 1920s and 1930s were a period of isolation from world affairs for the United States. The country drew inward and craved to return to what President Warren G. Harding had called normalcy. By cutting off the flow of European immigration, the nation's leaders hoped the country would become more homogeneous and placid.

Since northern Europe was favored under the new law, many northern Europeans came to America as part of the quota. But many more came illegally. Edmund Zech, a German sailor, jumped ship in Baltimore in 1926 and lived here for more than fifteen years before being discovered by immigration authorities. In an interview Zech said:

> I pulled a little stunt. . . . I told people I was from Madison, Wisconsin. Now I'll tell you why I said that. See, Madison, Wisconsin . . . I

was born June 2, 1903 . . . and in 1905 the town hall [in Madison] . . . burned down. All birth and death records . . . everything was destroyed. So no one could prove I was not born there. . . . And that's why I picked Madison, Wisconsin. Cause I studied the town. I could point out houses. I had names of people who lived there. Yet, I've never seen it. And in Madison, Wisconsin there were quite a few Germans there at the time. . . .

It was hard for me to get going here bein' that I had the handicap of [not being here] legally. You understand? If I'd been here legally, well I probably would have had a much better time. Then I could go . . . work where I wanted to go, which I could not. . . . And three times I had to beat it because the immigration [service] was after me. They came in the front door . . . I went out the back.[1]

Even if an immigrant came legally, America in the 1920s and 1930s could be a difficult place. The mid-twenties were a period of prosperity for the nation, but in 1929 the stock market crashed, and very shortly all Americans—native and foreign-born alike—found themselves in the midst of the worst depression in American history. Banks closed. Millions of people were out of work. And the country's economic system no longer seemed to be working. It was a desperate time.

Another sailor, Hans Koiuv, came to America

legally from Finland in 1922. He worked hard to make a new life for himself, only to see his dreams collapse with the onset of the Great Depression:

> We got a job and we worked 10 hours a day and when I say worked, we worked real hard and you know, the wages were $3.70 a day for 10 hour days. . . . Then I met the guy that told me that he's going to make a carpenter out of me, then you only work 8 hours a day and you got much better wages, so that kind of gave me the spirit to stay here and start to work up things. . . . When I learned the trade a little bit and had a steady job, it looked good to me compared to what you would have if you would stay and work in Finland because over there, especially those days, the wages were not so very big. . . .
>
> I stayed here and I got married here and then after I had been doing this here carpenter-contracting business for quite a few years . . . I had quite a little money already, so I figure if I'll buy a piece of ground and build my own houses and see if I can sell them. . . . But then the depression come and I got caught in it with a lot of houses on my hands and inside of a couple of years the prices of these houses went way down so I lose practically everything that I had.[2]

While the United States tried to remain isolated from world affairs, circumstances arose in Europe that made it impossible. Fascist dictatorships replaced democratic forms of government in Italy and Germany. And the United States could not isolate itself for long from the machinations of these military dictatorships. Of the two forms of fascism, the German variety, spawned by Adolf Hitler and his brown-shirted street gangs, was by far the more dangerous.

At the heart of Hitler's nazism was a virulent anti-Semitism that decreed that Jews, many of whose families had lived in Germany for centuries, were not true Germans but were, in fact, the enemies of all true Germans. Following his election as German chancellor in 1933, Hitler embarked on a course of persecution and destruction aimed at German Jews (and Jews in the countries Germany later conquered in World War II) that resulted in the worst systematic destruction of people the world had ever witnessed.

Thousands of Jews tried to leave Germany, but most countries were unwilling to accept the refugees. Even though German immigrants were favored under the United States immigration laws, the number of German Jews who wanted to flee Nazi Germany was so great that the quota could not accommodate them. Despite humanitarian pleas to relax the immigration laws, the United States government refused to increase the quota. Some German Jews made it to the United States, but they were only a fraction of those who wanted to enter.

One of the lucky few who came to the United

States from Nazi Germany was Helen Lange, a research technician at the University of Berlin, where her husband was a professor. In a recent interview Lange described the persecution she experienced in Germany, and how she and her family managed to reach the United States:

> The Hitler Laws—that means the laws of discrimination against Jews and other people who did not comply with the tenets and the ideology of National Socialism [nazism]—it started in the first of April 1933 and from [then] on— the ax of persecution followed one after the other. . . .
>
> The first Nazi law to come out against the Jews was that every Jew employed by a government or state agency or municipal agency had to be dismissed. And my husband, at that time my friend, was dismissed from his assistant professorship . . . and I was dismissed from [my job]. So we both suddenly found ourselves out of work.[3]

Lange and her fiancé, who was a doctor, went from job to job. For a time the Nazis allowed Jews to work for other Jews, while forbidding them to work in general industry. A new law declared that Jews had to wear a yellow Star of David at all times, and that Jewish store owners had to display the star on their places of business. For a Jew in Germany under Hitler, life

. . . was a continuous increase in terrorist acts of persecution against Jews. Especially in the smaller cities. . . . [where] they arrested Jews, they burned synagogues, they persecuted Jews, in the concentration camps where they had already come into being in 1933. . . .

I saw friends being taken into concentration camps. For instance, one . . . of my friends . . . was taken in a concentration camp. . . . Suddenly the Secret Police turn up and then arrested him and nobody knew why. He was a very harmless man, he was a gynecologist. He lived with his wife and his children in Berlin. And one day he was arrested and put into a concentration camp. Now, his wife tried to find out what the reason was. The reason wasn't given.[4]

In the midst of this chaos, Lange and her husband, whom she had married in 1936, gave little thought to fleeing Germany. They knew that their friends and relatives were being arrested, and that the Nazi persecutions would get worse, but Germany was their home.

We deluded ourselves for a great number of reasons which people who do not live under these circumstances do not understand. . . . We couldn't get out—because we didn't know anybody anywhere. We had no money outside the country. There was just no possibility to get out. So then you try to convince yourself that you can go on living the way it is. . . . You deny yourself reason. And that's just what it is. You become irrational . . . out of the will to live and not to be sucked in by despair, you delude yourself. . . .

For those who wanted to leave Germany, Hitler made increasing difficulties by not permitting them to take their money out. First of all, it was you could take only 50% out . . . [then] only 40% out. By . . . 1938 you could take out nothing. . . . Money had all to stay back in Germany. And then people said, "what can I do?"[5]

Lange and her husband applied for a visa to the United States. They had met a wealthy American in Germany who said he would sponsor them in America and lend them $15,000 to get started—vital assistance because under the immigration law, prospective immigrants had to prove that they would not end up on public assistance. Before the Langes' visa was approved, the Nazis tried to round up every Jew in Germany in one gigantic sweep known to history as "Crystal Night" because so many windows were broken. The Langes escaped the dragnet, and their visas were approved a month later. They left Germany with almost nothing, and arrived in New York on

January 12, 1939. It was an absolutely brilliant winter day. Very cold, very clear. The sky was

magnificent. One could see the outline . . . of
the New York coast from the boat. I will never
forget the exhilarating feeling—we were stand-
ing there at the tip of the boat, and see how
gradually the skyline of New York appeared. . . .

What was it on the boat emotionally? Full
of . . . expectation, of . . . marvelous feeling.
Safe from Germany. Safe. Safe. Safe. And looking in the beautiful unknown. . . . I felt that we
had escaped. I'm young. I have a profession.
I'm going to a free country, free from oppression. Free from restrictive laws, from thought
control.[6]

Throughout the 1930s thousands of Jewish and
non-Jewish refugees from fascism sought admission
to the United States. At first, the most urgent pleas
came from Germany. Then, as Hitler began to conquer other countries, pleas came from Czechoslo-
vakia, Poland, the Netherlands, Belgium, and
France. Unless they were lucky enough to receive a
quota number, all were refused.

The immigrants from Germany in the 1930s
were unusual in that an extraordinarily high percentage of them were college-educated professionals.
Many of them were prominent antifascist intellectuals and artists who had been purged from the
universities by the Nazis. So many skilled and
talented people were forced out of Germany—or put
to death in concentration camps—during the Nazi
era that one writer referred to it as German self-

mutilation. The list of political refugees from Germany included Bruno Walter and Otto Klemperer in music; Albert Einstein and Hans Bethe in physics; Thomas Mann, Stefan Zweig, and Bertolt Brecht in literature; Hannah Arendt and Hans J. Morgenthau in social science; Kurt Weill and Arnold Schönberg in music; Walter Gropius and Ludwig Mies van der Rohe in architecture; and Hans Hofmann and Piet Mondrian in painting.

The refugee intellectuals made a contribution to American life that was larger than their numbers would seem to indicate. Most obvious was their role in the development of the atomic bomb during World War II. Less obvious, but perhaps more important in the long run, was their influence on American cultural life. New ideas and new styles—especially in the arts—set in motion a blending of European and American ideas that led to a transformation of the American scene.

Most refugees, however, were average people, perhaps like the Langes a bit more educated than was usual for immigrants. These people saw America as a haven from the chaos that was enveloping the globe. But in America, too, they came face to face with Hitler's ideology.

Hitler preached that Germany was destined to rule the entire world. But Germany alone could not supply the 80 million to 100 million colonizing Germans that Hitler said would be needed for this job. Germans overseas and their descendants, no matter how long ago their families had left Germany, were expected to provide the manpower for Germany's plans of conquest. Early in the 1930s Hitler outlined his program to Herman Rauschning who quoted these conversations in his book *The Voice of Destruction:*

> I want to make it quite clear, too, that I make no distinction between German nationals and Germans by birth who are citizens of a foreign country. Superficially we shall have to make allowances for such citizenship. But it will be your special task to train all Germans, without distinction, unconditionally to place their loyalty to Germandom before their loyalty to the foreign state. Only in this way will you be able to fulfill the difficult tasks I shall give you.[7]

Not many German-Americans responded to this call, but enough were attracted by the notion that the German "Aryan" race was superior to form the German-American Bund. This organization emerged under the leadership of Fritz Kuhn, a German-born immigrant who had won the Iron Cross fighting in the German Army during World War I. The Bund tried to get German-Americans to become "race-conscious." It set up camps to indoctrinate young people in Nazi ideology and to give them para-military training.

The high point of Bund activity in the United States came in February 1939 when the German-American Nazis held a rally in Madison Square

Garden in New York City. The next day *The New York Times* reported:

> Protected by more than 1,700 policemen, who made of Madison Square Garden a fortress almost impregnable to anti-Nazis, the German-American Bund last night staged its much-advertised "Americanism" rally and celebration of George Washington's Birthday. . . .
>
> It was an enthusiastic audience that gave close attention to every speaker, and roared a mass response when called on to pledge allegiance to the flag. . . .
>
> Fritz Kuhn, national Fuehrer of the Bund movement since 1935 . . . declared that he and his followers were determined "to protect themselves, their children and their homes against those who would turn the United States into a bolshevik paradise."
>
> He denounced the "campaign of hate" he said was being waged against the organization in the press, the radio and the cinema "through the hands of the Jews."[8]

Most German-Americans were not won over. The Bund's most dramatic failures took place in the Midwest, the traditional heartland of German-American life and culture. In Milwaukee, for example, the Bund's activities were scorned by the *Milwaukee Journal*. The American Nazi organization found that it could not even hold secret meetings without reporters infiltrating them. And, indeed, there was something too ridiculous about men parading around in paramilitary uniform, professing to give undivided allegiance to the United States, while at the same time giving the Hitler salute to the American flag. The final blow to the Bund came with the trial and conviction of Fuehrer Kuhn for embezzling funds from the Bund.

When America finally entered World War II in December 1941, there was no outbreak of anti-German hysteria as had occurred during World War I. There were no demands that German-language instruction be stopped, that German music should be banned, or that sauerkraut be renamed "liberty cabbage." Something had changed between the two wars. Part of it was because of the reluctance among German-Americans to adopt the Nazi cause. And Germans in America were no longer as visible as they had been in 1917. The process of assimilation had been at work for a long time. Although traces of their cultural origins remained, older immigrant groups, especially German-Americans and Scandinavian-Americans found that a blending with American culture had been taking place. And it had a profound effect.

Chapter 15

Modern America

The Second World War left all of the northern European countries in ruins except Sweden, which had remained neutral throughout the war. France, Belgium, and the Netherlands were devastated. Germany was all but destroyed by the Allied invasions and the effects of years of massive bombings. And Denmark and Norway, both of which had been occupied by the Nazis, were left with deep wounds.

Shortly after the war ended, the United States developed a plan to help Europe to rebuild itself and to deter the spread of Communism. Named after General George C. Marshall, the financial aid sent to the war-damaged European countries under the Marshall Plan helped them to resume their normal place in world affairs. The United States lent the European countries $13 billion, and the assistance was put to good use. By the early 1950s, nearly all of Western Europe had once again become prosperous.

But the war left severe scars in Europe, and America became a beacon of hope to many affected by the war. Annemarie Schwartz was a child in a mountain town in western Germany during the Second World War. The memories of her childhood are filled with the privations of wartime, fears of bombing, and a great sense of relief when it was all over:

> During the war I was there and it was frightening. We were children, we didn't quite understand what went on. . . . Believe it or not, I didn't know for a long time that you get undressed when you go to bed. I thought you just opened your shoes. You know when there was an air raid you just had to be ready in seconds. . . .
>
> I remember when I started school I was six years old. I was four weeks in school and then the school is closed because the soldiers made it their own. And we had no school for a half a year. And then we went back to school again. And then the school was bombed. . . . So I practically missed at least three years of school.[1]

When American soldiers entered her village at the end of the war, Annemarie didn't know what to expect. The Americans were the ones who had been bombing the village, and she thought the soldiers would shoot her on sight.

> I never forget the night. . . . We were afraid to go outside our bungalow where we were sitting. And we came out, we saw those American soldiers. . . . All I remember is that we had to put our hands up over our heads and we were afraid to take them down because some guys would say if you take your hands down they gonna shoot you. . . .
>
> [The American soldiers] were all so simple and they walked so . . . relaxed comparing to the Germans . . . to the Nazis where ever they were . . . they always marched . . . you could hear them for miles away marching with the heavy boots . . . always looking straight on, no smile on their faces and so on. So in that way right away I liked them better. I said there must be something special, they must be different from German soldiers.[2]

Life in postwar West Germany was bleak for Annemarie Schwartz. She, and thousands of survivors of the war like her, dreamed of going to America to start a new life. Annemarie said:

> I wanted to have a better life. All I knew about Germany was bad things, bad memories. And I wanted to have . . . a better future in America. Work was easier you know, and more fair and so on. And so I wanted to come over here. . . .

I could never think of going back. . . . I'm
a little bit afraid of going back. I dream nights
that I'm back in Germany again and can't get
back to America no more. Maybe because I
don't have such good memories of Germany
and I see my children being so happy in their
childhood. And when I think back to my childhood I remember war. . . . and being frightened
day and night. And there's nothing to eat. And
you know little things like that.[3]

The postwar America that Annemarie Schwartz
came to was somewhat different from what America
had been after World War I. Then, the United States
had been wary of all immigration, and had passed
legislation that severely curtailed it. Following
World War II, the United States had emerged as one
of the most powerful nations on earth, and the leader
of the free world. The nation had assumed a respon-
sibility that meant relaxing its views on refugees,
coupled with aid schemes like the Marshall Plan.

But the United States was engaged in a cold war,
and this revived some of the old nativist sentiments.
When the FBI broke up a Communist spy ring that
had been sending United States atomic secrets to the
Soviet Union, its leader turned out to be a German
Communist agent named Claus Fuchs. Incidents like
these fueled what became known as the McCarthy
era in America, a time when anyone with leftist
political beliefs came under suspicion as a potential
Communist.

But if the cold war and the McCarthy era once again made Americans suspicious of foreigners, it was also a time when America led the Western world by example. When thousands of Germans from Communist East Germany fled to the West, for instance, the United States lent aid to West Germany for the refugees. After the East Germans constructed a wall dividing East and West Berlin in an attempt to stem the tide of refugees, President John F. Kennedy traveled to West Berlin and declared, "I am a Berliner." America was still a beacon of freedom.

Most of the refugees who came to the United States after World War II, however, were not northern Europeans. The great migrations from those countries to America were finished, and there seemed little likelihood that they would start again. Germany, Sweden, Norway, Denmark, France, and the Netherlands all developed advanced, industrialized economies after the war. Their standard of living is close to that of the United States. Their political systems leave room for dissenting points of view, and citizens of these countries no longer need seek a new land to practice their religious beliefs in peace. The reasons that compelled northern Europeans to leave their homelands for a new life in America for hundreds of years no longer exist.

Yet immigrants from northern Europe continue to come to the United States, although in much smaller numbers. Unlike the earlier immigrants, most of whom were drawn to the New World by economic necessity, the new immigrants seem to have different reasons, such as marriage to an American. In other cases, immigration may come about from the desire to move on and try something different.

Margaret Maryk moved to the United States from Sweden in 1958. Although she married an American whom she met here, she still retains her Swedish citizenship and goes back to Sweden once a year. She is typical of many northern Europeans who have emigrated.

> I don't know why [I left Sweden]. I didn't leave it because I was in misery. I didn't leave it because I didn't see any future in it. I didn't leave it because I didn't have anybody there. I left it to come back to it because I just wanted, maybe part of my Viking blood, you know, takes me out on adventures, and I just simply wanted to see something else. . . .
>
> The first time I arrived in this country was in 1958, middle of December, and I arrived in Los Angeles, and at that time there were no jets, so it took me 22 hours to get to the United States from Stockholm. It was, in a way, quite an experience just to set your foot in the sand just after leaving Stockholm in snow and arriving in Los Angeles, of course it was cold there according to their season, but to me it was the hottest summer day.[4]

Margaret Maryk still thinks of herself as Swedish. Today jet travel makes it possible for Maryk to visit Sweden often, to be part of life in America and Sweden at the same time—something that was impossible for immigrants before the invention of the airplane. As a result, she said:

> I cannot say I feel at home in a sense. I probably will not feel at home anywhere anymore. Once you have left someplace that actually was home, you took up something there, you tried to settle down here, but you can't—I can't completely feel that I didn't really pull up my roots completely there and I can't therefore plant it completely down here, so I feel I have one foot here, one foot there. . . .
>
> I was more Americanized the first three years I was in this country than I am now. I wanted to fit in more at that time, I didn't want to seem so foreign. I wanted to learn as much as I could about the American culture, the American people. I wanted to learn many of those things. Once I realized I probably would live here most of my life, I realized how important my Swedish background was to me and that I, in no way, wanted to lose it. I started to cultivate my traditions and things and felt that they were too important to me to let go.[5]

For Marte Walker coming to America from Norway was a rude shock:

I came over here in November 1963 from Stavanger, Norway. . . . It's a quiet town. It has got very narrow streets with the cobblestones downtown, and it has just small shops or stores and we got a harbor coming in over there, where the fishing boats used to come in all the time. . . . We could go down there and they used to come in with the boats, you used to buy fresh fish right from there . . . and there's a beautiful market down by the harbor there, that's got everything, vegetables and flowers and fruit. . . .

I met a guy over there and we got married over there. He was in Oceanographic Survey for the United States, and we came over here. . . . Of course it was exciting, you know, for the first time when I got to the United States, everything was so huge. I never seen all those skyscrapers and all that. I knew they were big but, you know, it's entirely different when you see them. The impression was that, oh God, don't let me get lost here because I'd never find my way back.[6]

At first Marte Walker found life in America to be exhilarating. Eventually, though, the hectic pace of American life caught up with her:

There was so many things you could do, like back in Norway there wasn't that many things you could do and over here there was everything, movies all over, you could go over to New York, you could do this and shows and it was unlimited what you could do here. But after a while . . . I don't know how to explain it, but it sort of wears off after a while and then . . . it becomes a little bit more like a hassle. . . . If you're going to go anyplace at all you gotta have a car. Like if you're going to the shopping center, you gotta have a car, the kids want to go to the library, you have to drive them there, they gotta go to school, you gotta drive them to school, it's back and forth, back and forth, I feel like a taxi driver all day. . . . Back home it was different. I think we did a lot more walking, you know, we weren't that spoiled with transportation.[7]

Although Marte Walker does not travel back to Norway, she feels she has not really parted with her native land. She lives in the United States, but her difficulty in adjusting makes her long for the simpler days of her youth.

I think I learned a lot more here than I would back home, about people and about life. I have learned much more, experienced a lot more than I would in Norway. . . . I learned so much during these years that I could never learn over there. I still have Norwegian citizenship, and I still consider myself Norwegian. Even if I become a United States citizen, . . . there would still be some of Norway in me, because you can talk to any, even old people . . . they still have it in their heart. I think it's with everybody. You could be the same if you went abroad and stayed abroad, you would say, America is the best, right?[8]

Marte Walker's mixed feelings about coming to live in America were probably shared by most northern European immigrants who left their native lands behind. Over the course of generations, however, their descendants became so much a part of American culture and society that they contributed in a large degree to making America what it is today.

Notes

Chapter 1.   Explorers and Visionaries

1. Quoted in Albert B. Hart, ed., *American History Told by Contemporaries,* Vol. 1 (New York: Macmillan & Co., 1896), p. 519.
2. Quoted in John A. Kouwenhoven, *The Columbia Historical Portrait of New York* (Garden City, N.Y.: Doubleday & Co., 1953), p. 29.
3. Quoted in Hart, *American History,* pp. 549–551.
4. Ibid.
5. Quoted in Oscar T. Barck, Jr. and Hugh T. Lefler, *Colonial America* (New York: The Macmillan Company, 1969), p. 170.

Chapter 2.   Aliens in an English World

1. Quoted in Louis B. Wright, *The Cultural Life of the American Colonies* (New York: Harper & Brothers, 1957), pp. 49–50.

190

2. Ibid.
3. Quoted in Maxine Seller, *To Seek America: A History of Ethnic Life in the United States* (Englewood, N.J.: Jerome S. Ozer, 1977), p. 31.
4. Quoted in Charles Dudley Warner, *Washington Irving* (Boston: Houghton Mifflin Co., 1881), pp. 211–212.
5. Quoted in Curtis P. Nettels, *The Roots of American Civilization* (New York: D. Appleton and Company, 1938), p. 386.
6. William Penn, "Some Account of the Province of Pennsylvania" (1681), in *Early Narratives of Pennsylvania, West Jersey, and Delaware* (New York: Charles Scribner's Sons, 1912), p. 274.
7. Penn, "A Further Account of the Province of Pennsylvania" (1685), in *Early Narratives,* p. 260.
8. Ibid.
9. Penn, "Some Account," in *Early Narratives,* p. 274.
10. Ibid., p. 276.

Chapter 3. From "Deutsch" to "Dutch"

1. Quoted in C. V. Wedgwood, *The Thirty Years War* (Garden City, N.Y.: Doubleday & Co., Anchor Books, 1961), p. 485.
2. Quoted in Hart, *American History,* pp. 559–561.
3. Quoted in Wayne Moquin, ed., *Makers of America,* Vol. 1 (Chicago: Encyclopaedia Britannica, 1971), pp. 211–213.
4. Ibid.
5. Quoted in Edith Abbott, *Historical Aspects of the Immigration Problem* (Chicago: University of Chicago Press, 1926), pp. 213–215.

6. Merrill Jensen, ed., *English Historical Documents to 1776* (New York: Oxford University Press, 1955), pp. 464–467.
7. Ibid.
8. Ibid.
9. Ibid., pp. 252–254.
10. Ibid.
11. Ibid.
12. Quoted in Abbott, *Historical Aspects,* pp. 415–416.

Chapter 4.   A New Nation
1. Quoted in LaVern J. Rippley, *The German-Americans* (Boston: Twayne Publishers, 1976), p. 32.
2. Ibid., p. 34.
3. Ibid., p. 36.
4. Quoted in Harold A. Larrabee, *Decision at the Chesapeake* (New York: Clarkson N. Potter, 1964), p. 75.
5. Ibid., p. 76.
6. Ibid., p. 80.
7. Max Ferrand, ed., *The Records of the Federal Convention of 1787,* Vol. 2 (New Haven: Yale University Press, 1937), pp. 216, 235–238.
8. Ibid.
9. Ibid.

Chapter 5.   Isolated and Cut Off
1. Quoted in Saul K. Padover, ed., *Thomas Jefferson on Democracy* (New York: New American Library, Mentor Books, 1967), pp. 107–108.

2. Quoted in Edwin Emery, *The Press and America* (Englewood Cliffs, N.J.: Prentice-Hall, 1962), p. 145.
3. *Annals of America,* Vol. 4 (Chicago: Encyclopaedia Britannica, 1968), pp. 59–61.
4. Ibid.
5. Ibid.
6. Ibid., pp. 49–50.
7. Quoted in Padover, *Thomas Jefferson,* p. 108.
8. Quoted in Virgil J. Vogel, *This Country Was Ours: A Documentary History of the American Indian* (New York: Harper and Row, 1972), p. 84.

Chapter 6. The Flood Begins

1. Quoted in Theodore C. Blegen, ed., *Land of Their Choice: The Immigrants Write Home* (Minneapolis: University of Minnesota Press, 1955), p. 15.
2. Quoted in John S. Lindberg, *The Background of Swedish Emigration to the United States* (Minneapolis: University of Minnesota Press, 1930), pp. 32–33.
3. Ibid., pp. 4–5.
4. Quoted in Blegen, *Land of Their Choice,* pp. 19–21.
5. Ibid., pp. 21–23.
6. Ibid., pp. 23–25.
7. Ibid., pp. 44–45.
8. Quoted in Leola N. Bergmann, *Americans from Norway* (Philadelphia: J. B. Lippincott Co., 1950), p. 50.
9. Quoted in George M. Stephenson, "When America

was the Land of Canaan," *Minnesota History,*
Vol. 10, 1929, p. 247.

10. Quoted in Abbott, *Historical Aspects,* pp. 56–59.

Chapter 7.   Travel to the New Land

1. Quoted in Carl Wittke, *We Who Built America*
(Cleveland: Press of Western Reserve University,
1964), p. 266.

2. Quoted in Lawrence Guy Brown, *Immigration:
Cultural Conflicts and Social Adjustments* (New
York: Longmans, 1933), pp. 85–86.

3. Ibid., p. 86.

4. Quoted in Henry S. Lucas, ed., *Dutch Immigrant
Memoirs and Related Writings,* Vol. 2 (Assen:
Van Gorcum & Co., 1955), pp. 88–89.

5. Ibid.

6. Quoted in Blegen, *Land of Their Choice,* pp. 104–
107.

7. Ibid.

8. Ibid.

9. Quoted in Friedrich Kapp, *Immigration and the
Commissioners of Emigration of the State of New
York* (New York: Nation Press, 1870), p. 67.

10. Quoted in Moquin, *Makers of America,* Vol. 3,
p. 17.

Chapter 8.   Settling on the Frontier

1. Quoted in Howard B. Furer, ed., *The Germans in
America, 1607–1970: A Chronology and Fact
Book* (Dobbs Ferry, N.Y.: Oceana Publications,
1973), pp. 106–107.

2. Ibid.

3. Quoted in Florence E. Janson, *The Background of Swedish Immigration* (Chicago: University of Chicago Press, 1931), p. 152.
4. Quoted in Bernard A. Weisberger, *The American Heritage History of the American People* (New York: American Heritage, 1971), pp. 154–155.
5. Quoted in Lucas, *Dutch Immigrant Memoirs,* pp. 184–185.
6. Ibid.
7. Quoted in Blegen, *Land of Their Choice,* pp. 166–167.
8. Quoted in Vogel, *This Country Was Ours,* p. 132.
9. Quoted in Blegen, *Land of Their Choice,* pp. 427–428.

Chapter 9. Settling in the Cities

1. Edward Bok, *The Americanization of Edward Bok: The Autobiography of a Dutch Boy Fifty Years After* (New York: Charles Scribner's Sons, 1922), pp. 434–435.
2. Quoted in Isaac A. Hourwich, *Immigration and Labor: The Economic Aspects of European Immigration to the United States* (New York: G. P. Putnam's Sons, 1912), pp. 232–233.
3. Jacob R. Marcus, ed., *Memoirs of American Jews,* Vol. 3 (Philadelphia: Jewish Publication Society, 1955), pp. 34–37.
4. Ibid.
5. Ibid.
6. Ibid.
7. Quoted in Furer, *The Germans in America,* pp. 126–127.
8. Ibid.

9. Quoted in Brown, *Immigration,* p. 93.
10. Quoted in Furer, *The Germans in America,* pp. 117–118.
11. Quoted in Emily Balch, *Our Slavic Fellow Citizens* (New York: Arno Press and the New York Times, 1969), p. 414.

Chapter 10.   Reaction and Rebellion
1. Quoted in Abbott, *Historical Aspects,* pp. 503–511.
2. Thomas R. Whitney, *A Defense of the American Policy as Opposed to the Encroachments of Foreign Influence* (New York: DeWitt & Davenport, 1865), pp. 307–315.
3. Quoted in Stanley Feldstein and Lawrence Costello, eds., *The Ordeal of Assimilation: A Documentary History of the White Working Class* (New York: Doubleday & Co.; Anchor Books; 1974), pp. 147–151.
4. Ibid.
5. Quoted in Weisberger, *American Heritage History,* p. 174.
6. Frederick Bancroft, ed., *Speeches, Correspondence, and Political Papers of Carl Schurz,* Vol. 1 (New York: G. P. Putnam's Sons, 1913), p. 48.
7. Ibid., pp. 49–50.
8. Ibid., pp. 71–72.
9. Quoted in Moquin, *Makers of America,* Vol. 3, pp. 163–164.
10. Ibid., pp. 161–162.
11. Quoted in Lucas, *Dutch Immigrant Memoirs,* pp. 257–261.

Chapter 11. Immigration in the Gilded Age

1. "Fair Wages," by "A Striker," *The North American Review,* Vol. 125, No. 258, (Sept.–Oct. 1877), pp. 322–326.
2. Ibid.
3. Quoted in Samuel Yellen, *American Labor Struggles* (New York: Harcourt, Brace & Co., 1936), pp. 47–48.
4. Ibid., pp. 52–54.
5. Quoted in Moquin, *Makers of America,* Vol. 4, pp. 116–119.

Chapter 12. The Huddled Masses

1. Quoted in Claude M. Fuess, *Carl Schurz, Reformer* (New York, Dodd, Mead & Co., 1932), p. 1.
2. Frederick Bancroft and William A. Dunning, eds., *The Reminiscences of Carl Schurz,* Vol. 3 (New York: McClure's, 1908), pp. 257–262.
3. Ibid.
4. Quoted in Albert Bigelow Paine, *Thomas Nast: His Period and His Pictures* (New York: The Macmillan Company, 1904), p. 179.
5. Ibid., p. 203.
6. Jacob A. Riis, *The Making of an American* (New York: The Macmillan Company, 1901), p. 69.
7. Ibid., p. 267.
8. Ibid., pp. 272–273.
9. Ibid., pp. 309–310.

Chapter 13. One Hundred Percent Americanism

1. Interview with Hjordis Mortenson in *They Chose America, Conversations with Immigrants,* Vol. 2,

An Audio Cassette Program (Princeton: N.J.: Visual Education Corporation, 1979).

2. Quoted in Richard O'Connor, *The German-Americans, An Informal History* (Boston: Little, Brown, 1968), pp. 381–382.

3. Ernest L. Meyer, *"Hey! Yellowbacks!" The War Diary of a Conscientious Objector* (New York: John Day, 1930), pp. 12–13.

4. Quoted in Moquin, *Makers of America,* Vol. 7, p. 123.

Chapter 14. Between the Wars

1. Interview with Edmund Zech in *They Chose America.*

2. Interview with Hans Koiuv in *They Chose America.*

3. Interview with Helen Lange in *They Chose America.*

4. Ibid.

5. Ibid.

6. Ibid.

7. Quoted in O. John Rogge, *The Official German Report: Nazi Penetration, 1924–1942* (New York: Thomas Yoseloff, 1961), p. 30.

8. Quoted in Furer, *The Germans in America,* pp. 135–136.

Chapter 15. Modern America

1. Interview with Annemarie Schwartz in *They Chose America.*

2. Ibid.

3. Ibid.

4. Interview with Margaret Maryk in *They Chose America.*
5. Ibid.
6. Interview with Marte Walker in *They Chose America.*
7. Ibid.
8. Ibid.

Suggested Reading

Abbott, Edith. *Historical Aspects of the Immigration Problem.* Chicago: University of Chicago Press, 1926.

Annals of America, Vol. 3. Chicago: Encyclopaedia Britannica, Inc., 1968.

Balch, Emily. *Our Slavic Fellow Citizens.* New York: Arno Press, 1969.

Bancroft, Frederick, ed. *Speeches, Correspondence, and Political Papers of Carl Schurz,* Vol. 1. New York: G. P. Putnam's Sons, 1913.

Bancroft, Frederick, and William A. Dunning, eds. *The Reminiscences of Carl Schurz,* Vol. 3. New York: McClure's, 1908.

Barck, Oscar T., Jr., and Hugh T. Lefler. *Colonial America.* New York: The Macmillan Company, 1969.

Bergmann, Leola N. *Americans from Norway.* Philadelphia: J. B. Lippincott Co., 1950.

Blegen, Theodore C., ed. *Land of Their Choice: The Immigrants Write Home.* Minneapolis: University of Minnesota Press, 1955.

Bok, Edward. *The Americanization of Edward Bok: The Autobiography of a Dutch Boy Fifty Years After.* New York: Charles Scribner's Sons, 1922.

Brown, Lawrence Guy. *Immigration: Cultural Conflicts and Social Adjustments.* New York: Longman's, 1933.

Emery, Edwin. *The Press and America.* Englewood Cliffs, N.J.: Prentice-Hall, 1962.

"Fair Wages" by "A Striker," *The North American Review,* Vol. 125, No. 258 (Sept.–Oct., 1877).

Feldstein, Stanley, and Lawrence Costello, eds. *The Ordeal of Assimilation: A Documentary History of the White Working Class.* New York: Doubleday & Co., Anchor Books, 1974.

Ferrand, Max, ed. *The Records of the Federal Convention of 1787,* Vol. 2. New Haven: Yale University Press, 1937.

Fuess, Claude M. *Carl Schurz, Reformer.* New York: Dodd, Mead & Co., 1932.

Furer, Howard B., ed. *The Germans in America, 1607–1970: A Chronology and Fact Book.* Dobbs Ferry, N.Y.: Oceana Publications, 1973.

Hart, Albert B., ed. *American History Told by Contemporaries,* Vol. 1. New York: Macmillan & Co., 1896.

Hourwich, Isaac A. *Immigration and Labor: The Economic Aspects of European Immigration to the United States.* New York: G. P. Putnam's Sons, 1912.

Janson, Florence E. *The Background of Swedish Immi-

gration. Chicago: University of Chicago Press, 1931.

Jensen, Merrill, ed. *English Historical Documents to 1776.* New York: Oxford University Press, 1955.

Kapp, Friedrich. *Immigration and the Commissioners of Emigration of the State of New York.* New York: Nation Press, 1870.

Kouwenhoven, John A. *The Columbia Historical Portrait of New York.* Garden City, N.Y.: Doubleday & Co., 1953.

Larrabee, Harold A. *Decision at the Chesapeake.* New York: Clarkson N. Potter, 1964.

Lindberg, John S. *The Background of Swedish Emigration to the United States.* Minneapolis: University of Minnesota Press, 1930.

Lucas, Henry S., ed. *Dutch Immigrant Memoirs and Related Writings.* Assen: Van Gorcum & Co., 1955.

Marcus, Jacob R., ed. *Memoirs of American Jews,* Vol. 3. Philadelphia: Jewish Publication Society, 1955.

Meyer, Ernest L. *"Hey! Yellowbacks!" The War Diary of a Conscientious Objector.* New York: John Day, 1930.

Moquin, Wayne, ed. *Makers of America,* 10 vols. Chicago: Encyclopaedia Britannica Educational Corporation, 1971.

Nettels, Curtis P. *The Roots of American Civilization.* New York: D. Appleton and Company, 1938.

O'Connor, Richard. *The German-Americans, An Informal History.* Boston: Little, Brown and Company, 1968.

Padover, Saul K., ed. *Thomas Jefferson on Democracy.*

New York: New American Library, Mentor Books, 1967.

Paine, Albert Bigelow. *Thomas Nast: His Period and His Pictures.* New York: The Macmillan Company, 1904.

Penn, William. "A Further Account of the Province of Pennsylvania" (1685), in *Early Narratives of Pennsylvania, West Jersey, and Delaware.* New York: Charles Scribner's Sons, 1912.

Penn, William. "Some Account of the Province of Pennsylvania" (1681), in *Early Narratives of Pennsylvania, West Jersey, and Delaware.* New York: Charles Scribner's Sons, 1912.

Riis, Jacob A. *The Making of an American.* New York: The Macmillan Company, 1901.

Rippley, LaVern J. *The German-Americans.* Boston: Twayne Publishers, 1976.

Rogge, O. John. *The Official German Report: Nazi Penetration, 1924–1942.* New York: Thomas Yoseloff, 1961.

Seller, Maxine. *To Seek America: A History of Ethnic Life in the United States.* Englewood, N.J.: Jerome S. Ozer, 1977.

Stephenson, George M. "When America Was the Land of Canaan," in *Minnesota History,* Vol. 10, 1929.

They Chose America, Conversations with Immigrants, An Audio Cassette Program, 2 vols. Princeton, N.J.: Visual Education Corporation, 1979.

Vogel, Virgil J. *This Country Was Ours: A Documentary History of the American Indian.* New York: Harper & Row, 1972.

Warner, Charles Dudley. *Washington Irving.* Boston: Houghton Mifflin Co., 1881.

Wedgwood, C. V. *The Thirty Years War*. Garden City, N.Y.: Doubleday & Co., Anchor Books, 1961.

Weisberger, Bernard A. *The American Heritage History of the American People*. New York: American Heritage, 1971.

Whitney, Thomas R. *A Defense of the American Policy as Opposed to the Encroachments of Foreign Influence*. New York: DeWitt & Davenport, 1865.

Wittke, Carl. *We Who Built America*. Cleveland: Press of Western Reserve University, 1964.

Wright, Louis B. *The Cultural Life of the American Colonies*. New York: Harper & Brothers, 1957.

Yellen, Samuel. *American Labor Struggles*. New York: Harcourt, Brace & Co., 1936.

A Brief History of U.S. Immigration Laws

The authority to formulate immigration policy rests with Congress and is contained in Article 1, Section 8, Clause 3 of the Constitution, which provides that Congress shall have the power to "regulate commerce with foreign nations, and among the several States, and with the Indian tribes."

Alien Act of 1798: authorized the deportation of aliens by the President. Expired after two years.

For the next seventy-five years there was no federal legislation restricting admission to, or allowing deportation from, the United States.

Act of 1875: excluded criminals and prostitutes and entrusted inspection of immigrants to collectors of the ports.

Act of 1882: excluded lunatics and idiots and persons liable to becoming public charges.

First Chinese Exclusion Act.

Acts of 1885 and 1887: contract labor laws, which made it unlawful to import aliens under contract for labor or services of any kind.

(Exceptions: artists, lecturers, servants, skilled aliens in an industry not yet established in the United States, etc.)

205

Act of 1888: amended previous acts to provide for expulsion of aliens landing in violation of contract laws.

Act of 1891: first exclusion of persons with certain diseases; felons, also persons having committed crimes involving moral turpitude; polygamists, etc.

Act of 1903: further exclusion of persons with certain mental diseases, epilepsy, etc.; beggars; also "anarchists or persons who believe in, or advocate the overthrow by force or violence of the Government of the United States or of all government or of all forms of law or the assassination of public officials." Further refined deportation laws.

Acts of 1907, 1908: further exclusions for health reasons, such as tuberculosis.

Exclusion of persons detrimental to labor conditions in the United States, specifically Japanese and Korean skilled or unskilled laborers.

Gentlemen's Agreement with Japan: in which Japan agreed to restrictions imposed by the United States.

Act of 1917: codified previous exclusion provisions, and added literacy test. Further restricted entry of other Asians.

Act of 1921: First Quota Law, in which approximately 350,000 immigrants were permitted entry, mostly from northern or western Europe.

Act of 1924: National Origins Quota System set annual limitations on the number of aliens of any nationality immigrating to the U.S.

"Gigolo Act" of 1937: allowing deportation of aliens fraudulently marrying in order to enter the United States either by having marriage annulled or by refusing to marry once having entered the country.

Act of 1940: Alien Registration Act provided for registration and fingerprinting of all aliens.

Act of 1943: Chinese Exclusion Acts repealed.

Act of 1945: War Brides Act admitted during the three years of act's existence approximately 118,000 brides, grooms, and children of servicemen who had married foreign nationals during World War II.

Act of 1949: Displaced Persons Act admitted more than four hundred thousand people displaced as a result of World War II (to 1952).

Act of 1950: Internal Security Act excluded from immigrating any present or foreign member of the Communist party, and made more easily deportable people of this class already in the U.S. Also provided for alien registration by January 10 of each year.

Act of 1952: Immigration and Nationality Act codified all existing legislation; also eliminated race as a bar to immigration.

Acts of 1953–1956: Refugee Relief acts admitted orphans, Hungarians after 1956 uprising, skilled sheepherders.

1957: special legislation to admit Hungarian refugees.

1960: special legislation paroled Cuban refugees into the U.S.

Act of 1965: legislation amending act of 1952 phased out national origins quotas by 1968, with new numerical ceilings on a first come, first served basis. Numerical ceilings (per annum): 120,000 for natives of the Western Hemisphere; 170,000 for natives of the Eastern Hemisphere. New preference categories: relatives (74 per cent), scientists, artists (10 per cent), skilled and unskilled labor (10 per cent), refugees (6 per cent).

Act of 1977: allowed Indo-Chinese who had been paroled into the U.S. to adjust their status to permanent resident.

1979: presidential directive allowed some fourteen thousand Vietnamese "boat people" to enter the U.S.

Index